John Edward Gray

A revision of the genera and species of Viverrine animals

Founded on the collection in the British Museum

John Edward Gray

A revision of the genera and species of Viverrine animals
Founded on the collection in the British Museum

ISBN/EAN: 9783741130489

Manufactured in Europe, USA, Canada, Australia, Japa

Cover: Foto ©Thomas Meinert / pixelio.de

Manufactured and distributed by brebook publishing software
(www.brebook.com)

John Edward Gray

A revision of the genera and species of Viverrine animals

Cetaceans, the Right Whale (*Balæna mysticetus*) and the Narwhal (*Monodon monoceras*) are well known to inhabit the Spitzbergen seas. Mr. Malmgren, in his careful paper before alluded to, enumerates six or perhaps seven species of Whales, not reckoning a Porpoise. We therefore have seven or eight Cetaceans, seven Carnivores (including *Ursus maritimus*, on which I have no remark to make), and one Ruminant as the sum total of the Mammalian fauna of Spitsbergen. Without extending these notes by going into details, I may here state that I think the bird-fauna cannot be reckoned at more than twenty-seven species. We therefore have the singular result of a country, say as large as Ireland, where the number of Mammalian bears to the number of Ornithic species the ratio of 15 or 16 to 27.

13. A Revision of the Genera and Species of Viverrine Animals (Viverridæ), founded on the Collection in the British Museum. By Dr. J. E. Gray, F.R.S.

Having received from Dr. Meller a Viverrine animal from Eastern Africa which appeared to be new, I was induced to compare it with the specimens in the Museum. Here I found two specimens received in 1855 from M. Verreaux of Paris, under the name of *Herpestes mutgigella* of Rüppell from Eastern Africa, quite different from, and three or four times as large as the adult animals of that species which were received from Dr. Rüppell as type specimens—besides another different species from the same part of the world, which we purchased of M. Parzudaki, also under the name of *Herpestes mutgigella*.

Being desirous of determining these species and some other unnamed specimens with accuracy, I was induced to reexamine all the specimens of the skins and osteological preparations that are in the British Museum, very many of which are the original specimens on which many species have been described; and as the materials grew under my hand into an essay on the species of the tribe, I have sent it to the Society in the hope that it may assist to elucidate the numerous species of this group of carnivorous Mammalia.

The *Viverridæ* include a considerable number of the middle-sized and small Carnivora. They are all natives of the Old World—that is to say, Africa and Asia (one of the species spreading itself over some of the southern parts of Europe)—except the genus *Bassaris*, which inhabits Mexico.

The greater number of the species are found in Africa, and several are confined to Madagascar; others are inhabitants of various parts

This fact I unfortunately had not noticed until my return home; so that (Porpoises being in general of so common occurrence on a sea voyage) I neglected to record, as I otherwise should certainly have done, the dates and localities of their appearance. It is of course possible that what I took to be Porpoises were only the young of some larger Cetacean; but I do not think this was the case.

of Asia. Some species of the genera, as here revised, come from Africa, and others from Asia; but I do not know of any species but *Viverricula malaccensis* which is common to the two sections of the Old World.

The essential character of the Viverridæ is to have two tubercular grinders on each side of the upper jaw, and one on each side of the lower. In the genera *Linsang* and *Poiana* the hinder upper tubercular grinder is absent, and the teeth agree in number with those of the genus *Felis*; but the shape of the skull and teeth show that they belong to this family. In *Crossarchus* and *Suricata* the lower hinder grinder is absent; and in some species of the genera, where these teeth are present, they are often reduced to a very small size. There are generally three false grinders before the flesh-tooth; but in some genera the front one, which is often very small, is entirely wanting, or sometimes falls out early.

Mr. Waterhouse, in the 'Proceedings of the Zoological Society' for 1839, in a paper "On the Dentition of Carnivora," observes, "The *Viverridæ* have the same form of skull as the *Canidæ*, but differ in having the posterior portion more produced; the long palate is carried farther back, and the small back molar, observable in the lower jaw of the Dog, is here wanting. They have, therefore, but one true molar on either side of the lower jaw, and two true molars on each side of the upper jaw." The form of the palate here relied on is not found in all the genera of the family, and sometimes varies in genera which are very nearly allied both in external characters and dentition.

The Hyæna, Mr. Waterhouse was inclined to regard as an aberrant form of Viverridæ. Its carnassier has a large inner lobe, and in this respect also resembles the Viverra's, and not the Cat's.

(See also some observations by me on the change of the teeth, &c., in some of the genera, in a paper in the 'Proceedings of the Zoological Society' for 1832, pp. 32, 62.)

There can be no doubt that the skull affords very important characters, especially for the division of the species into groups or genera, and also for the distinction of the species; but no one can examine an extensive series of skulls, even of animals obtained from the same locality, without being struck with the variation the skull presents during the growth and age of the animal, and also the variation which the specimens of the same age present, showing that the skull and the teeth are quite as liable to vary in form in each species (within certain limits, these limits being different in the various species) as any other part of the animal; so that a species cannot be said to be firmly established until the external form, the bones, and the habit of the species have been carefully studied, distinctly showing that the labours of the palæontologist in a zoological point of view are very unsatisfactory, from the necessary want of material for forming a reliable determination of species.

The late Mr. Turner made some very interesting observations on the base of the crania of the Carnivora, with a new distribution of the genera (see Proc. Zool. Soc. 1848, p. 63). It is to be regretted that he died so young, and could not continue his researches; for I have no doubt he would have thrown great light on the structure of the skulls of this group, as he always followed my studies like a shadow. Thus when I published my "Arrangement of the Hollow-horned Ruminants' in 1846 (Ann. N. H. xviii. p. 227), he shortly after read his paper on their skulls (see Proc. Zool. Soc. 1850, p. 164); when I commenced the study of the species of Edentata by a monograph of *Bradypus* in Proc. Zool. Soc. 1849, p. 65, he read his paper on the skull of Edentata in 1851. Being an observant and careful osteologist, he observed many particulars that a general zoologist would have overlooked; but this limitation of his study confined his views; so that he would not allow such genera as *Saiga*, *Pantholops*, or *Tamandua* (which have such striking external characters), because he did not observe such differences in the skulls as he considered of generic importance.

The impulse that Cuvier gave to zoology by the study of the skeletons and teeth of Mammalia, as shown in the 'Ossemens Fossiles,' made such an impression on the succeeding students of zoology, that most of them, overlooking the importance that Cuvier himself attached to external characters, have confined themselves far too exclusively to the characters offered by these parts, overlooking the fact that bones and teeth are liable to vary like other parts of the animal, and that characters in the teeth that may be of great importance in most groups may be of comparatively little value in the others. Thus in the *Paradoxuri*, which every one must allow form a very natural group, well characterized by its habits as well as its external character, the skulls and the flesh-teeth offer such variations in form in the different species that they would be considered as good generic characters in any other tribe of Viverridæ.

The notes on the skull and teeth in this paper are always taken from those of the adult animal, unless it is stated to the contrary.

The Viverridæ have been divided into many genera, some only containing a single species, while one or two other genera have been left as magazines containing a number of heterogeneous species which had not been particularly examined. The characters of some of the published genera have not been made out on any uniform plan. Indeed that is the system of the day, to search out some animal which has some striking character, and to form it into a genus, leaving the greater number of species in the family under the old generic denomination, which, when examined with care, have quite as distinct characters. This is an evil which requires remedying, and I have tried to obviate it by submitting all the species of the group to the same kind of revision as M. Geoffroy submitted the old species when he rearranged the collection in the Jardin des Plantes more than half a century ago.

M. Temminck, in the 'Esquisses Zoologiques,' p. 100, has inquired if *H. widdringtonii* is a species or a local variety. He had never seen the animal; but this shows the spirit in which he seems always to have looked on the species described by others which were not in his museum. In the same work he gives a short *résumé* of the species of the genera *Herpestes* and *Paradoxurus*, and states that the catalogues are encumbered with many double and triple *emplois*, which must be erased from the systematic catalogue. After citing some examples of species which have been described nearly simultaneously by zoologists living in distant countries, as *H. urinator*, *H. paludosus*, *H. penicillatus*, and *Cynictis steedmani* (which certainly are not instances deserving much blame, especially when we consider the many cases in which M. Temminck himself has described species in Holland which had been long previously described in England), he proceeds to propose to unite some species which are, in my opinion, perfectly distinct (some even belonging to different sections of the genus) according to characters that are almost universally adopted, and which he himself uses in other places. In the revision of the genus *Paradoxurus* in his monograph, and again in the above work, he has united together species which have not the slightest relation to each other, and which he never could have united if he had seen authentic specimens of them. Thus he unites *P. grayi*, *P. nipalensis*, and *P. laniger* to *P. larvatus*, and *P. crossi* and *P. pallasii* to *P. musanga*, regarding *P. bondar* as separate. Now if he had united *P. grayi*, *P. nipalensis*, *P. laniger*, *P. crossi*, and *P. bondar* together, he would have had the excuse that they all have some similarity of external appearance; and he might have been misled if he had only casually looked at them through the glass of the cases in the museum, as he looked at some specimens which he says he saw when in England. Synonyms cannot be determined by such an examination, nor is science advanced by such assertions.

M. Temminck was an eminent ornithologist, and has studied some groups of Mammalia, perhaps not with so much success. He was an amiable naturalist, but has carried his political anglophobia (so well seen in his 'Essay on the Dutch Colonial Possessions') into his zoological studies. This blinded him to the labours of the zoologists of this country, the richness of our collection, and thus rendered his observations in regard to their work not worthy of attention, as they otherwise might have been. It is to be observed that he never had a regular scientific training, never attempted to form scientific specific characters, and is rather to be regarded as a patron and amateur than as a scientific zoologist. He was the first in his country, as the late Earl of Derby was in this.

The arrangement of the genera of Viverridæ into natural groups is not easy; for though they naturally place themselves together in a certain kind of order, the difficulty is to find a character that is common to the genera that appear to be most related to each other.

I published an arrangement of the genera of this family then known, according to the characters afforded by the hairiness and baldness of the sole of the hind feet, in the 'Proceedings of the Zoological Society' for 1832, p. 63, which is well adapted for the purpose, though, like other arrangements, it is not infallible, nor to be used too strictly, or it will separate genera naturally allied to each other.

The continued study of the subject has shown me several other characters which I had before overlooked. I propose the following arrangement as one which seems best adapted to exhibit the natural affinities of the genera, as far as they can be shown in a linear series, and as one that will enable the student to determine the species. Thus, for example, I would propose to divide the tribes characterized in the paper (in the 'Proceedings of the Zoological Society') above referred to into two groups, according to the form and the hairiness of the toes and the form of the claws, characterized by the foot and claw of the Cat and of the Dog or the Bear.

The bones of the toes of the animals of the first group, as in the Cats, form an angularly arched line, the last phalanges being bent up, so that the animal when it walks does not blunt its claws, which are only exserted when it wants to catch or tear some other animal. In the second group, which I have called *Dog-footed*, the bones of the toes form a more or less extended, slightly arched line; and the claws, being always exposed, and worn when the animal walks, are more or less blunt at the end. The more typical Dog-footed animals often scratch holes in the ground; and some have strong elongated arched claws for the purpose.

The groups are well defined and very distinct, and the above characters are well marked in most of the genera; but some few genera have feet that seem nearly intermediate between the two groups. In such cases the whole appearance of the animal must be taken into consideration, and the genera placed with those to which they seem most allied in habit and manners.

The difference in the form of the foot and claws is common to three families of the Carnivora; and, as it is connected with considerable peculiarity in the habit of the animal, it forms a good character to separate the tribes and genera into groups, thus:—

VIVERRIDÆ.	URSIDÆ.	MUSTELIDÆ.
A. *Toes arched; claws acute, retractile.*		
Æluropoda.	*Dendropoda.*	*Acanthopoda.*
Viverrina.	Ailurina.	Mustelina.
Genettina.	Cercoleptina.	Lutrina.
Paradoxurina.	Procyonina.	
B. *Toes straight; claws exserted, blunt.*		
Cynopoda.	*Brachypoda.*	*Platypoda.*
Herpestina.	Ursina.	Mephitina.
Mungosina.		Mydaina.
		Melina.

The genera of the three other families of Carnivora have a uniform kind of foot. Thus the *Felidæ* have a hairy foot, curved toes, and sharp claws; and the *Canidæ* and *Hyænidæ* straight toes and exserted, blunt claws.

The animals of the different families which have sharp retractile claws have habits in common. Thus the Cats, the Genets, the *Paradoxuri*, the Martins, the *Ailuri*, and the *Cercoleptæ* defend themselves by lying on their back and using both the hind and front feet to claw with; they walk softly, and jump on their prey.

The animals with exserted claws generally scratch the ground into holes, and defend themselves with their front feet; and some, as the Suricate and the Bears, sit on their haunches; and the Bear, the Coatimondi, the Raccoon, &c. use their fore feet as hands to take their food, as well as in defence.

Synopsis of the Genera.

I. The Cat-footed (*Æluropoda*). *The toes curved, arched, hairy, webbed; claws sharp, retractile.*

A. Typical. Digitigrade. *The underside of the feet hairy, except the pads, metatarsus, and sometimes a small part of the tarsus. Upper flesh-tooth elongate; upper tubercular grinder small, transverse. Nose short; underside flat, with a central groove.* Viverracea.

1. *Body robust; tubercular grinders* 2/1, 2/1; *back of tarsus hairy.* Viverrina.

PROTELES. Legs elongate; front longest. Head short, broad; ears long. Tail short, bushy. An anomalous genus allied to *Hyæna*.

VIVERRA. Legs moderate, equal. Head elongate. Tail conical, ringed. Back crested. Orbit of skull incomplete.

BASSARIS. Tail cylindrical, ringed. Legs equal, moderate. Back not crested. Orbit of skull incomplete.

VIVERRICULA. Legs moderate, equal. Tail conical, ringed. Back not crested; heel with a small bald spot. Orbit of skull complete.

2. *Body robust; tubercular grinders* 2/1, 2/1; *underside of the tarsus with a narrow naked streak.* Genettina.

GENETTA. Back with a black subcrectile streak.

FOSSA. Back without any central streak.

3. *Body slender, elongate; tubercular grinders* 1/1. Prionodontina.

POIANA. Back of tarsus with a narrow naked streak.

PRIONODON. Back of tarsus hairy.

B. Aberrant. Subplantigrade. *The underside of the toes and more or less of the back of the tarsus naked, callous. Flesh-tooth strong, upper tubercular grinders large, broad.*

1. *Nose produced; underside convex, hairy, without any central longitudinal groove; hinder part of the tarsus bald, callous. Face produced.* Cynogalina.

CYNOGALE. Tail short, cylindrical.

2. *Nose short, underside flat, with a central groove.*

a. *The hinder part of the tarsus hairy to the palm ; the tail bushy.* Galidiina.

GALIDIA.

b. *The upper part of the hinder part of the tarsus hairy ; tail ringed.* Hemigalina.

HEMIGALEA.

c. *The hinder part of the tarsus bald, callous.*

* *Tail thick, strong, prehensile.* Arctictidina.

ARCTICTIS.

** *Tail very long, subconvolute ; frenum naked, glandular ; head elongate.* Paradoxurina.

PARADOXURUS. Flesh-tooth elongate, triangular ; tubercular teeth oblong. Orbit very incomplete.

PAGUMA. Flesh-tooth short, triangular, large. Orbit very imperfect.

ARCTOGALE. Flesh-tooth triangular, small. Orbit nearly complete. Palate very narrow, elongate.

NANDINIA. Flesh-tooth elongate, triangular ; tubercular teeth triangular, transverse. Orbit rather incomplete. Palate narrow, short.

*** *Tail long, bushy ; head short, broad ; frenum hairy ?* Cryptoproctina.

CRYPTOPROCTA.

II. The Dog-footed (*Cynopoda*). *The toes elongate, separate, more or less hairy ; claws exserted, blunt ; feet narrow, underside bald or only covered with short hairs. Orbit of skull complete, or nearly complete, behind.*

A. *Nose short ; underside flat, with a central groove.* Herpesteacea.

1. *Head elongate, conical ; tail conical or cylindrical.* Herpestina.

* *Front claws elongate, compressed ; back streaked.*

GALIDICTIS. Toes 5–5. Tail subcylindrical, covered with long hair. Back striped.

** *The front claws short, compressed ; back grizzled ; flesh-tooth long, narrow.*

HERPESTES. Toes 5–5. Tail conical, with long hair. Teeth moderate.

ATHYLAX. Toes 5–5. Tail conical, with long hair. Teeth very large.

Calogale. Toes 5–5. Tail cylindrical, elongate, covered with shortish hairs; tip pencilled.

Galerella. Toes 5–4. Tail cylindrical, elongate, covered with short hair.

** *The front claws short, compressed; flesh-tooth broad, triangular.*

Calictis. Toes 5–5. Tail conical, with long hairs. Back grizzled. Pupil oblong, transverse.

Ariela. Toes 5–5. Tail elongate, subcylindrical. Back cross-banded.

Ichneumia. Toes 5–5. Legs rather high. Tail conical, bushy. Back grizzled.

? Bdeogale. Toes 4–4. Legs moderate. Tail conical, bushy. Back grizzled. Soles hairy?

*** *Front claws elongate, produced; tail conical, with long hair; back grizzled.*

Urva. Toes 5–5. Head elongate. Soles of hind feet hairy. False grinders 3/4.

Tæniogale. Toes 5–5. Head elongate. Soles of hind feet bald. False grinders 3/4.

Onychogale. Toes 5–5. Head elongate. Soles of hind feet hairy. Front claws very long. False grinders 3/4.

Helogale. Toes 5–5. Nose short. False grinders 2/3. Body slender. Soles bald.

2. *Head short, ventricose; tail bushy, expanded laterally; claws elongate.* Cynictidina.

Cynictis. Toes 5–4.

B. *Nose produced; underside convex, hairy, without any bald central groove.* Rhinogaleacea.

1. *Head elongate; nose short; teeth 40; false grinders 3/4.* Mungosina.

Rhinogale. Tail conical. Toes 5–5. Front claws short.

Mungos. Tail conical. Toes 5–5. Front claws elongate.

2. *Head ventricose; nose elongate; teeth 36; false grinders 3/3, 3/3.* Crossarchina.

Eupleres. Toes 5–5. Claws short, hooked. Hind soles hairy.

Crossarchus. Toes 5–5. Claws hooked. Hind soles bald.

Suricata. Toes 5–4. Claws elongate, slender. Hind soles hairy.

The shortness of the characters that I give to some genera has been objected to by some writers, especially by amateurs who have not studied the Linnean brevity and method of description. They overlook the fact that the characters of the sections and subsections of the family that precede the genus form an essential part of the generic character, in the same manner that the section of the genus is part of the specific character of the species that the section contains. The definition of the subsections of the families and genera requires more study, analysis, and consideration than the writing out of a long generic character, that contains particulars that are common to a number of allied genera, such as the writers who make the complaint usually give. At the same time, the use of such detailed characters requires a greater exertion on the reader's part to eliminate the essential particulars, which are the real characters of the group. In the above table, the most easily seen and often empirical characters are purposely chosen, for facility of use and brevity. I have even used the colour of the animal for this purpose; for it has a great influence on the formation of a natural genus—more than many zoologists are willing to admit. Even those who know this fact avoid making use of it, apparently fearing that it might not be considered scientific! In the body of the essay, longer generic characters are given. Those who object to analytic characters forget the immense number of animals now known, and the great advantage of a rapid way of discovering the name of the animal they seek, and whose history they desire to know. As Mr. W. S. Macleay justly observes, "the modern art of describing is too long, often insufferably long, while human life remains as short as ever."—*Illust. Zool. South Africa*, p. 54.

I. The Cat-footed Viverridæ (*Æluropoda*)

have broad feet, with short arched toes, covered with abundant close-spreading hair, united together at the base by a more or less distinct web, and armed with short, sharp, retractile claws. They are covered with a soft elastic fur, except the anomalous genus *Arctictis*, which has a very harsh fur and a prehensile tail.

A. Digitigrade. *The underside of the hind feet hairy, except the pads of the toes, the metatarsus, and sometimes a small part of the tarsus; the upper flesh-tooth elongate; upper tubercular small, transverse; nose short, underside flat, with a central groove.*

Tribe 1. Viverrina.

The body robust; tubercular teeth 2/1, 2/1; the back of the hind feet hairy, except the pad of the toes and the metatarsus.

There is a deep pouch for secreting civet, in the form of a deep cavity on each side of the anus (P. Z. S. 1832, p. 63).

All the genera of this tribe are restricted to the Old World, except *Bassaris*, which is American. This American group is peculiar in having two tubercles on the inner lobe of the flesh-tooth, while this tooth in all the other genera has only a single lobe on the crown of that process of the tooth.

1. PROTELES.

Head short, broad; muzzle truncated; ears long and pointed. The body short; neck and back crested; legs elongate, front longest; tail short, bushy. Toes 5—4. Teeth 32; false grinders $\frac{1-1}{1-1}$; tubercular grinders 2/1. Looks like a small Hyæna, with the teeth of a Civet.

Proteles, I. Geoff. Mém. Mus. ii. 370, 1824; Ann. Sci. Nat. viii. 252; A. Smith, S. Afr. Q. Journ. i. 48.

PROTELES CRISTATUS. B.M.

Proteles cristatus, Gray, Cat. Mam. B. M. 47; Gerrard, Cat. Ost. B. M. 70.

P. lalandii, I. Geoff. Mém. Mus. xi. 370, t. 20; Mag. Zool. 1841, i. t. 30; Fischer, Syn. Mamm. 195; Schinz, Syn. Mamm. i. 424.

Viverra cristata (*Grey Jackal*), Sparrm. Voy. ii. 177.

P. typicus, A. Smith, S. A. Q. J. i. 48.

Viverra ? hyænoides, Cuvier, MS.; Desm. Mamm. 538.

P. hyænoides, Blainv.

Genette hyenoïde, Cuv. Oss. Foss. iv. 388.

Proteus, Edinb. Phil. Journ. ii. 103.

Hyæna Genet, Griffith, A. K. t.

Hab. S. Africa: Cape (called "Nadron"); Natal (*A. Smith*), ("Aard Wolf").

"Female lighter; under fur less abundant."—*A. Smith.*

2. VIVERRA.

Viverra, Linn.; Gray, P. Z. S. 1832, p. 63.

Head long; muzzle acute; pupil oblong, vertical. Neck with large black and white marblings. Body short, compressed; back black-crested; legs moderate, equal; tail moderate, tapering, ringed. Toes 5—5; claws semiretractile. Teeth 40; false grinders $\frac{3-3}{3-3}$.

Hab. Africa and Asia.

* *Tail black.* African.

1. VIVERRA CIVETTA. B.M.

Tail black; sides spotted.

Viverra civetta, Schreb. Säugeth. t. 111; A. Smith, S. A. Q. J. i. 44; Bennett, Tower Menag. 99, fig.; Gray, Cat. Mamm. B. M. 47; Gerrard, Cat. Ost. B. M. 70; Schinz, Syn. Mamm. i. 361; Temm. Esq. Zool. 88.

Civette, Buffon, ix. 299, t. 34.

Var.? *Viverra poortmanni*, Pucheran, Rev. et Mag. Zool. vii. 154, 1853; Arch. der Naturg. 1856, p. 44.

Hab. Africa: Abyssinia; Fernando Po (*Thompson*); Guinea (called "Kaukaus") (*Temm.*); Gaboon (*Aubry Le Comte*).

** *Tail black, ringed.* Asiatic.

2. VIVERRA ZIBETHA. B.M.

Tail ringed.

Viverra zibetha, Linn. S. N. i. 65; Fischer, Syn. Mamm. 168; Gray, Illust. Ind. Zool. ii. t. 5; Proc. Zool. Soc. 1832, p. 63; Cat. Mamm. B. M. 47; Gerrard, Cat. Ost. B. M. 71; Schinz, Syn. Mamm. i. 362; Horsfield, Cat. Mus. India House, 54.

Meles zibethica, Linn. S. N.

Viverra undulata, Gray, Spic. Zool. t. 8.

V. civettoides, V. melanurus, V. orientalis, Hodgson, J. Asiatic Soc. Bengal, x. 909.

Zibet, Buffon, ix. 299, t. 31.

Hab. Asia: Bengal (*Horsfield*); India (*Hardwick*); Calcutta (*Oldham*); Nepal (*Hodgson*); China (*J. Reeve*); Formosa (*Swinhoe*); ? Isle of Negros (*Cuming*) (skull B.M.); ? Malay peninsula (*Horsfield*).

Skull elongate, narrow. Nose compressed. Orbit incomplete behind. Teeth very like *Genetta*; upper hinder tubercular small, oblong, transverse, with two outer and one large inner tubercle. Lower jaw shelving in front; lower edge rather arched, without any tubercles below the end of the tooth-line; the tubercular grinders subcircular, with three lobes on the crown.

3. VIVERRA TANGALUNGA. B.M.

Tail black above, and ringed on the lower side.

Viverra tangalunga, Gray, P. Z. S. 1832, p. 63; Cat. Mamm. B. M. 48; Cantor, Mamm.; Horsfield, Cat. Mus. India House, 57.

Viverra zibetha, Raffles, Linn. Trans. xiii. 231; F. Cuvier, Mam. Lithog. t.

Hab. Sumatra (called "Tangalung") (*Raffles*); Borneo, Celebes, Amboyna (*Müller*); Malayan peninsula (*Cantor*).

What is *Viverra megaspila*, Blyth, Journ. Asiat. Soc. Bengal, 1862, p. 321?

3. BASSARIS.

Bassaris, Licht. Isis, 1831, p. 510.

Body elongate; back not crested. Legs moderate, equal. Tail elongate, bushy, dark-ringed. Toes 5—5, separate; claws acute. Teeth 38; false grinders $\frac{2-2}{3-3}$; tubercular grinders $\frac{2-2}{2-2}$.

Hab. Mexico.

BASSARIS ASTUTA. B.M.

Fur grey.

Bassaris astuta, Licht. Isis, 1831, p. 510; Darst. Säugeth. t. 42;

Gray, Cat. Mam. B. M. 50; Gerrard, Cat. Ost. B. M. 72; Baird, Mamm. N. Amer. t. 74. f. 2; Mexico, 13; Eydoux, Voy. Bonite, t. (skeleton); De Blainv. Ostéogr. Viverra, t. 12 (teeth).

Tepe maxthalon, Hernand, Voy. Fav. t. 4 & 18.

Var. *fulvescens*. Far more fulvous, perhaps of a different season. B. M.

Bassaris sumichrasti, De Saussure, Rev. et Mag. de Zool. 1860, p. 5, t. 1.

Hab. Mexico (called "Cat Squirrel," often domesticated) (*Phillips*).

Skull ovate, rather produced in front, more compressed. Orbits large, incomplete behind; lower edge confluent with the zygomatic arch; zygomatic arch slender, short, and much bowed out. The brain-case swollen; the contraction rather in front of the hinder edge of the orbit. The teeth normal. False grinders 2/4, 2/4, the upper compressed, second without any internal lobe. The flesh-tooth triangular; inner lobe broad, on the inner side of the front edge, with two distinct conical tubercles; outer side about one-third longer than the front margin. The tubercular grinders large, rather broader than long, with four small tubercles on the outer and three on the inner side; inner edge rounded; the hinder tubercular oblong, transverse, like the former one, but smaller. The lower jaw shelving in front; the lower edge arched; the tubercular grinders large, oblong, longitudinal, with two large tubercles on the front and two smaller in an oblique line on the hinder part of the crown. Length of skull $3\frac{1}{4}$ inches; width of the brain-case $1\frac{1}{3}$ inch, of the zygomatic arch $2\frac{1}{12}$ inches.

De Saussure's figures represent the animal as if it were spotted, and the tail with only a few broad rings.

4. VIVERRICULA.

Viverricula, Hodgson, Journ. Asiat. Soc. Beng. x. 909.

Head tapering. Throat with lunate dark bands. Body elongate; back not crested. Legs moderate, equal. Tail almost as long as the body, tapering, dark-ringed. Toes 5—5; claws acute, compressed. Pupil oblong, vertical. Teeth 40; false grinders $\frac{3-3}{3-3}$; flesh-tooth longer than broad in front, inner lobe on the front margin; tubercular grinders $\frac{2-2}{2-2}$.

Hab. Asia.

Like a Genet, but with hairy soles to the feet, a shorter tail, and no crest. Foot with a small bald spot on the side of the palm-pad (see Hodgson, J. A. S. B. t. 31. f. 8).

VIVERRICULA MALACCENSIS. B.M.

Grey; back with seven black or dark streaks more or less broken up into spots; shoulders, sides, and legs spotted; feet deep brown and black; tail with seven or eight black rings.

Viverricula malaccensis, Cantor, Cat. Mam. Malay. 29.

Viverra malaccensis, Gmelin, S. N. 92 (from Sonn.); Gray, Cat. Mamm. B. M. 48; Gerrard, Cat. Ost. B. M. 70.

V. gunda, Hamilton, Buchanan, Icon.

V. rasse, Horsf. Zool. Java, t.; P. Z. S. ii. (1832), p. 23; Schinz, Syn. Mamm. i. 362.

V. indica, Geoff. MS.; Fischer, Syn. Mamm. 171; Desm. Mamm. 210; Gervais, Mag. Zool. 1835, p. 10, t. 19; Horsf. P. Z. S. ii. (1832) p. 23.

? *V. bengalensis*, Gray, Illust. Ind. Zool. i. t. 4.

V. leveriana, Shaw, Mus. Lever. t. 21.

Genetta manillensis, Eydoux.

G. indica, Lesson, Man. 174.

Genette rasse, F. Cuvier, Mamm. Lithogr. t.

Civette de Malacca, Sonnerat, Voy. ii. 144, t. 91.

Viverricula indica, Hodgson, Journ. Asiat. Soc. Beng. x. 909; Calcutta J. N. H. ii. 47.

Var. (paler spots less distinct). *Viverra pallida*, Gray, Proc. Zool. Soc. ii. 63; Illust. Ind. Zool. ii. t. 6; Cat. Mam. B. M. 48; Gerrard, Cat. Ost. B. M. 71; Swinhoe, P. Z. S. 1862.

Hab. Asia; Madras (*Elliot*); Gangootra, Nepal (*Hodgson*); Java (*Horsfield*).

Dr. Horsfield believed there were two species combined under this name (see Proc. Zool. Soc. ii. 23, 1832):—

V. rasse. Back with eight *broad* longitudinal lines; the three lateral lines on each side interrupted and obscure.

V. indica. Back with eight *narrow* longitudinal lines; the lateral lines continued.

I formerly thought that *V. pallida* from China, in which the spots and stripes are very indistinct, might be different; but a series of specimens from different localities seems to show a gradation from one to the other.

This species differs very much in colour from different localities and perhaps in different seasons. The stripes and spots are sometimes very black and distinct; at others, as in *V. pallida*, they are very indistinct, scarcely to be distinguished from the general colour of the fur.

The skull elongate, compressed; nose compressed. The orbit imperfect behind, confluent with the temporal fossæ. Grinders:—false 3/4, 3/4; front upper small, compressed; the third rather thicker, without any internal lobe; the flesh-tooth trigonal, oblique, elongate, half as long again as the width on the front margin—the internal lobe trigonal, on the inner side of the front edge; the front tuberculars trigonal, outer side oblique; front edge rather wider than the length of the outer margin; the hinder tubercular subcircular, with three lobes. The lower jaw slender; lower edge slightly curved, without any prominence under the end of the tooth-line; the tubercular grinders subcircular, with three nearly equal lobes.

Length of skull $3\frac{3}{4}$ inches; width of brain-case $1\frac{1}{6}$ inch, at zygomatic arches $1\frac{3}{4}$ inch.

I wrote to my excellent friend Dr. Peters to inquire if the *Tunga* of Anjuan could be the *V. fossa*, and if it was not a *Genetta*. He assured me that it agrees in all particulars with the Indian *V. rasse*, and, "like it, has no bald streak along the sole. It has a hairy sole to the hind feet, and a small callous spot to the pads of the palms towards the heel."—*Letter*, 24th Nov. 1864.

Dr. Peters regards the animal called the *Tunga*, which is common on the island of Anjuan, one of the Comoro Islands, near Madagascar, on the east coast of Africa, as the same as the *Viverra rasse* of Dr. Horsfield: he says it agrees with it in colour, in the form of the ears, and in the bristly quality of its fur; and it has the soles of its feet covered with hair as in that animal. He also observes that the fauna of these islands agrees more with those of Madagascar and India than with that of continental Africa (see Peters, Reise nach Mossamb., Mammalia, 113). If the animal is identical, it is the only species of the family I know common to Asia and Africa.

Tribe 2. GENETTINA.

The body robust; tubercular grinders 2/1, 2/1; the underside of the tarsus of the hind feet with a narrow bald line extending from the pads nearly to the heel. The orbit of the skull is very imperfect, only contracted above. The fur is soft, spotted or cloudy, and the tail ringed.

5. GENETTA, Cuv. Mamm. Lithog.

Genetta, Brisson, R. A. 252; Gray, P. Z. S. ii. (1832) p. 63.

Viverra, § *Genetta*, Cuvier, R. A.; Gray, Proc. Zool. Soc. 1832; Cat. Mamm. B. M. 49.

The body elongate; back with a broad, continued, more or less crested, black streak. Tail long, slender, hairy, ringed. Legs moderate. Feet hairy. Toes 5—5; the sole of the hind foot with a narrow longitudinal bald streak. Claws short, retractile. Skull elongate, narrow. Teeth 40; false grinders $\frac{3-3}{4-4}$; flesh-tooth elongate; tubercular grinders $\frac{2-2}{1-1}$.

Hab. Africa and South Europe.

Sir A. Smith observes, "They strike and scratch with the fore feet, like a cat. They spring on their prey, and climb with great facility."

The form and colour of the tail seem the best characters for the distinction of the species; the pale bands even vary a little in width and distinctness. The form, colour, and disposition of the spots vary much; they are sometimes confluent.

* *Tail tapering, with elongate, rather spreading hairs, and with numerous black and white rings; tip white.*

1. GENETTA VULGARIS. B.M.

Blackish grey, black-spotted; tail elongate, with white and black rings of nearly equal length, the tip whitish; vertebral line black, subcristate; the fore legs and the feet grey, black-spotted; the hind legs black behind near the hock.

Genetta vulgaris, Gray, P. Z. S. ii. (1832) p. 63; Lesson, Man. 173; Gerrard, Cat. Ost. B. M. 71.

Viverra maculata, Gray, Zool. Misc. 9, t. 9; A. Smith, S. African Quart. Journ. ii. 136.

G. afra, F. Cuv. Mamm. Lithogr. t.

Viverra genetta, Linn.; Fischer, Syn. Mamm. 169.

Genetta bonapartei, Loche, Mag. Zool. 1857, t. 18.

Hab. South Europe, North Africa, and Asia: in B. M., from Nismes (*Verreaux*); Madrid, Algiers (*Loche*); Tangiers (*Favier*); Barbary (*Gray*); Asia, Mount Carmel (*Tristram*).

The length of the rings varies in different specimens, depending on the length of the hairs of the tail. In some, two or more of the rings are more or less confluent, especially on the upper part and near the end of the tail.

I cannot find any difference between the specimens from Europe, Algiers, Tangiers, and Mount Carmel. The distinctness and darkness of the streak upon the forehead differs in specimens from the same localities.

2. Genetta felina. B.M.

Blackish grey, black-spotted; vertebral line black; tail elongate, white-and-black ringed, rings of nearly equal length; tip whitish; the outer side of the fore and hind legs black; feet blackish.

Genetta felina, Gray, Proc. Zool. Soc. ii. (1832) p. 63; Cat. Mamm. B. M. 49; A. Smith, S. A. Quart. Journ. i. 47.

Viverra felina, Thunb. Sv. Akad. xxxii. 166, t. 7; Fischer, Syn. Mamm. 170; Temm. Esq. Zool. 92.

G. vulgaris?, A. Smith, S. Afr. Quart. Journ. ii. 45.

Hab. South Africa: Cape of Good Hope (*Verreaux*) (the Musk-cat of the colonist); Latakoo, common (*A. Smith*).

The chief difference between this and *G. vulgaris* is that the legs and feet are blacker, the head is darker, with a more distinct black streak up the forehead between the eyes.

Genetta rubiginosa, Pucheran (Rev. et Mag. de Zool. vii. 1855, 154; Arch. für Naturg. 1856, p. 44:—

"*Griseo-albescens, fulvo lavata, maculis dorsalibus fere toto rubiginosis; cauda ad basim quatuor annulis rubiginosis, quatuor deinde nigris prædita.*

"*Hab.* Cape of Good Hope"—*J. Verreaux*), is probably the same.

3. Genetta senegalensis. B.M.

Pale yellowish grey, brown-spotted; vertebral line black, subcristate behind; tail elongate, slender, yellow-and-black ringed, the pale rings the longest; tip of tail pale; the hinder part of the hind legs blackish or dark brown.

Genetta senegalensis, Gray, P. Z. S. ii. (1832) p. 63; Cat. Mamm. B.M. 49; Gerrard, Cat. Oss. B. M. 71.

Viverra senegalensis, Fischer, Syn. 170 (from F. Cuv.); Temm. Esq. Zool. 92.

Genette de Sénégal, F. Cuv. Man. Lith. t. .

?*Genetta aubryana*, Pucheran, Rev. et Mag. de Zool. vii. (1855) p. 154; Arch. für Naturg. 1856, p. 44.

Fossane, Brown, Illust. t. 43.

Hab. West Africa: Senegal (*Verreaux*); ? Gaboon (*Aubry le Comte*); Sennaar (*Brit. Mus.* 46, 6, 15, 43). East Africa: Abyssinia (*B. M.* 44, 5, 17, 27); Dongola (*B. M.* 46, 9, 2, 27). North Africa (*B. M.* 43, 12, 28, 2).

Skull tapering in front; nose compressed. Orbit very large, very incomplete behind; the zygomatic arch confluent with the lower edge of the orbit, moderate. False grinders 3/4, 3/4; upper rather far apart, front small, second compressed, with a small lobe on each end; third compressed, with a small lobe on the middle of the inner side and one at the hinder end. The flesh-tooth triangular, much longer than the breadth at the front edge, with a moderate-sized internal lobe rather behind the front inner angle. The tubercular grinders trigonal, with a sloping outer edge; the front twice as wide as long on the outer edge; the hinder small. The lower jaw slender, erect, with a shelving chin or short symphysis and a curved lower edge without any tubercles under the end of the tooth-line; the tubercular grinder roundish, with two large anterior lateral and a similar-sized posterior central lobe. Length of skull $3\frac{1}{6}$ inches; width of brain-case $1\frac{1}{12}$, at zygoma $1\frac{5}{6}$.

***Tail subcylindrical, with shortish fur; end black, with imperfect rings; tip black, base with alternate, equally long, black and white rings.*

4. Genetta tigrina. B.M.

Grey brown, with black spots, the larger more or less brown in the centre; the hind feet darker; the tail elongate, cylindrical, black, with rather broad white rings, narrower than the black one; tip of tail black.

Genetta tigrina, Gray, Cat. Mamm. B. M. 49; Gerrard, Cat. Ost. B. M. 71; A. Smith, S. Afr. Q. Journ. i. 46.

Viverra tigrina, Schrb. Säugeth. t. 115; Fischer, Syn. Mamm. 170.

Genetta vulgaris, Rüppell.

G. amer, Rüppell; Gray, Cat. Mamm. B. M. 49.

G. abyssinica, Rüppell, Fauna Abyss. t. 11.

Viverra abyssinica, Gerrard, Cat. Oss. B. M. 71; Schinz, Syn. Mamm. i. 364.

Viverra genetta, Peters, Mossamb. Mamm. 113.

Hab. South Africa: Cape of Good Hope (the Musk-cat of the colonists); Natal and East Africa (*Verreaux*); Mozambique (*Peters, Kirk*); Abyssinia (*Rüppell*).

*** *Tail subcylindrical, with shortish fur, black; middle part with some imperfect rings beneath, the base with a few narrow white rings.*

5. Genetta pardina. The Berbe. B.M.

Fur reddish grey brown, with black spots more or less brown in the centre; the feet and hinder part of hind legs brown; tail elongate, covered with shortish hairs, with narrow pale or reddish rings on the basal half, black at the end, with very indistinct narrow or pale rings.

Genetta pardina, I. Geoff. Mag. Zool. 1832, t. 8; Gray, Cat. Mamm. B.M. 50; Temm. Esq. Zool. 93.

Genette pantharine, F. Cuvier, Mamm. Lithogr. t.

Genetta poënsis, Waterhouse, Proc. Zool. Soc. 1838, p. 59 (from a flat skin); Schinz, Syn. Mamm. i. 366.

Viverra genettoides, Temm. Esq. Zool. 89, 1853?

Genetta fieldiana, Du Chaillu, Proc. Boston N. H. Soc. vii. (1860) p. 302; Gray, Ann. & Mag. N. H. viii. 60; Arch. f. Naturg. 1862, p. 128 (from the Gaboon).

G. servalina, Pucheran, Rev. et Mag. de Zool. vii. (1855) p. 154; Arch. für Naturg. 1856, p. 44.

Berbe, Bosmann, Voy. Guinea, 31. f. 5; Buffon, H. N. xiii.

Hab. Fernando Po (*Waterhouse*); Guinea (*Temm.*); Gaboon (*Du Chaillu*); West Africa (*B.M.*); interior of Senegal (*I. Geoffroy*).

The specimens vary considerably in the size of the spots; in some they are brown with black edge, in others almost uniformly black; but I can see no characters by which they can be separated.

Genetta poënsis seems to be the same variety as that described by I. Geoffroy and M. Du Chaillu.

6. Fossa.

The back without any black subcrested vertebral streak; the soles of the hind feet hairy, with ———?

Fossa daubentonii.

Viverra fossa, Schreb. Säugeth. t. 114 (from Buffon); Fischer, Syn. Mamm. 170; Schinz, Syn. Mamm. i. 369.

Genetta fossa, Gray, P. Z. S. 1822; A. Smith, S. Afr. Q. Journ. i. 46; Lesson, Mamm. 174; Pucheran, Ann. & Mag. N. H. 1855, p. 41.

Fossane, Buffon, H. N. xiii. 163, t. 20.

Hab. Madagascar (*Mus. Paris.*).

" Fur grey black, rufous-varied, a white spot over the hinder angle of the eye; back and nape with black lines, four of which extend from the nape to the tail, continuous to the middle of the back, and the last of their length broken into very close spots; the sides, shoulders, and thighs with spots placed in three lines on each side; lips, chin, and beneath dirty white; tail with many narrow half-rings, of a reddish colour, which do not extend to the lower side;

feet yellowish white. Length of body and head 17 inches; of tail 8½ inches. There are no subcaudal glands.

"*Hab.* Madagascar (*Poivre, Mus. Acad. Sci.* 1761)."—*Buffon, H. N.* xiii. 163, t. 21.

I do not know any other description of this species; that of all other authors, including Dr. A. Smith, is a mere copy of the above. There does not appear to be any central dorsal stripe, so characteristic of the Genets; the soles of the front feet have not been described.

Tribe 3. Prionodontina.

Body slender, elongate; limbs very short; tubercular grinders 1/1; *fur soft, close, erect; the tail very long, cylindrical, ringed.*

7. Prionodon.

Prionodon (subgenus of *Felis*), Horsf. Java, Hodgson.

Linsang, Gray, Cat. Mamm. B. M. 48; Müller, Zool. Ind. Arch.

Body very slender; back not crested. Legs short. Tail very long, cylindrical, dark-ringed. Toes 5—5. Claws very acute. Skull elongate. Teeth 38; false grinders $\frac{3-3}{3-3}$; flesh-tooth elongate; tubercular grinders $\frac{1-1}{2-2}$.

Hab. Asia and Africa.

1. Prionodon gracilis. B.M.

Fur white; back with broad black cross bands; sides of neck with a broad black streak continued along the sides, confluent with the bands of the back; back of neck with five parallel black streaks. Tail with seven black and white streaks; a second streak, broken into spots, from the side of the neck to the haunches. Legs with small black spots.

Linsang gracilis, Müller, Zool. Ind. Arch. i. 28, t.; Gray, Cat. Mamm. B. M. 48; Gerrard, Cat. Ost. B. M. 72.

Viverra? linsang, Hardw. Linn. Trans. xiii. 256, t. 24; De Blainv. Ostéogr. t. 12 (teeth).

Felis (*Prionodon*) *gracilis*, Horsf. Zool. Java, t.

Viverra hardwickii, Lesson, Man. 172 (not Gray).

V. genetta, Deschamps, MS. B.M.

Paradoxurus prehensilis, Schinz, Cuv. Thierr. iv. 349.

Viverra gracilis, Desm. Mamm. 539; Schinz, Syn. Mamm. i. 363.

Paradoxurus linsang, Fischer, Syn. Mamm. 159, 1829.

Hab. Asia: Malacca?, Siam?, Sumatra?, Java? (*Horsfield*).

2. Prionodon pardicolor. B.M.

Pale whitish grey; back of neck and shoulders with three streaks, diverging from the vertebral line; back with two series of large square spots; the shoulders, sides, and legs with round black spots; an elongated spot on the middle of the front part of the back, between the square spots on the sides of the body.

Prionodon pardicolor, Hodgson, Calcutta Journ. N. H. ii. 37, t. 1. f. 3 & 6, 1841.

Linsang pardicolor, Gray, Cat. Mamm. B. M. 49; Gerrard, Cat. Ost. B. M. 72.

Viverra perdicator, Schinz, Syn. Mamm. i. 366 (misprint).

Hab. Nepal.

The skull elongate; nose rather short, compressed; brain-case narrow in front, swollen over the ears, and contracted and produced behind. Orbits not defined behind, confluent with the temporal cavity; zygomatic arch slender. Palate contracted behind. Teeth 38; upper false grinders compressed; flesh-tooth narrow, much longer than wide in front; the outer edge three-lobed, inner tubercle on the front edge; tubercular grinders transversely trigonal, much wider than long, the outer edge sloped, and the hinder lobes in the middle of the hinder edge. There is no hinder tubercular; but the one present is quite like the front tubercular in the typical Viverridæ.

The skulls of the two species are very similar; but the skull is rather larger, the palate narrower in front and behind, and the bullæ of the ears are narrower and less ventricose in *P. gracilis* than in *P. pardicolor*.

The following are the measurements in inches and twelfths in *P. gracilis*:—length of skull 1″ 7‴; width at brain-case 11‴; width of zygomatic arch 1″ 3½‴; length of nose 9‴. *P. pardicolor*:—length of skull 2″ 6‴; width of brain-case 10½‴; width of zygomatic arch 1″ 2½‴; length of nose 8½‴.

8. Poiana.

Head small; ears rounded. Body slender, elongate; fur soft, close, short, nearly uniform in length, spotted; no central dark vertebral line. Legs rather short. Feet hairy, cat-like; toes 5—5, short; hind soles covered with hair; with a short narrow naked line, forked below, and only reaching to the middle of the foot above. Claws retractile. Tail cylindrical, black-ringed.

Hab. Africa.

Very like *Prionodon* in external appearance, but with the feet of *Genetta*.

Poiana richardsoni. B.M.

Pale brown, black-spotted; spots on the back larger, square; spots on sides and feet smaller, rounded.

Linsang richardsoni, Gerrard, Cat. Ost. B. M. 72.

Viverra genettoides, Temm. Esq. Zool. 89, 1853?

Genetta richardsoni, Thompson, Ann. N. H. 1842.

Genetta poënsis (jun.), Waterh. P. Z. S. 1838, p. 59.

Hab. West Africa: Fernando Po (*Thompson*); Guinea (*Temm.*).

Skull and teeth very like *Prionodon*; but the brain-case is ovate and more ventricose. The orbits not defined behind, and confluent with the temporal cavity; zygomatic arch stronger. The nose is compressed. The palate is very narrow behind. Teeth 38; the upper false grinders compressed; the flesh-tooth considerably longer than broad in front, with a roundish inner lobe on the front edge, separated from the other lobe by a notch; the tubercular grinders transverse, triangular, broad, with a small lobe in the middle of the hinder edge. There is no second tubercular grinder in the upper jaw. Length of skull 2″ 9‴, of nose 9‴; width of brain-case 11‴, of zygomatic arch 1″ 5‴.

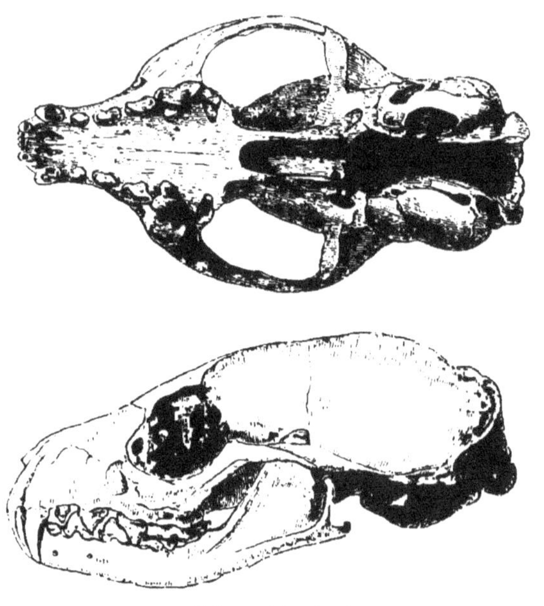

Poiana richardsoni.

B. Aberrant Cat-footed Viverridæ. *Subplantigrade. The underside of the toes and more or less of the back of the tarsus near the foot bald and callous. The flesh-tooth is massive and strong; the tubercular grinder large, broad.*

1. *Nose produced, convex, and hairy beneath, without any central longitudinal groove. The orbit of the skull only slightly defined above.*

Tribe 4. CYNOGALINA.

The toes short, covered with dense hairs, slightly webbed at the base; the claws short, compressed, retractile; the soles of the hind feet broad, bald for about two-thirds of their length; the heel hairy. The nose rather produced, with a bald muzzle, convex, and hairy beneath, without any central groove. The frenum covered with hair. The fur very dense, close, erect, soft, and elastic. Tail short, cylindrical.

9. Cynogale.

Cynogale, Gray, Mag. N. H. 1836, i. 579; Proc. Zool. Soc. 1836, p. 86; Cat. Mamm. B. M. 53.

Lamictis, De Blainv. Compt. Rend. 1837, 56.

Potamophilus, S. Müller, Zool. Ind. Arch. 103, 1839.

Head elongate. Nose broad, swollen; under side hairy, without any central groove. Ears small, rounded, covered with short hairs. Whiskers rigid, elongate, and some longer; more rigid bristles under the ears and over the eyes. Tail much shorter than the body, cylindrical, covered with short hair like that of the body; frenum covered with hair. Teeth 40; false grinders 3/3, 3/3; tubercular grinders 2/2, 2/2.

Cynogale bennettii. B.M.

Cynogale bennettii, Gray, Mag. Nat. Hist. i. 579, 1836; Proc. Zool. Soc. 1836, p. 86; Cat. Mamm. B. M. 53; Eydoux & Soul. Voy. Bonite, t.; Gerrard, Cat. Ost. B. M. 78; De Blainv. Ostéogr. Viverra, t. 12 (teeth).

Viverra (Lamictis) carchanas, Jourdan, Ann. Sci. Nat. viii. 281, t. 8 *a*, 1837; De Blainv. Ann. Sci. Nat. xiii.

Potamophilus barbatus, S. Müller, Zool. Ind. Arch. t. 17.

Cynogale barbata, Schinz, Syn. Mamm. i. 388.

Hab. Borneo (*Honeywood*).

Skull elongate; face much produced, compressed; orbits not defined at all behind, confluent with the zygomatic cavity; zygomatic arch strong; forehead between the orbits very narrow. Teeth 40; canines compressed; false grinders compressed, third without any inner lobe; flesh-tooth triangular, largely tubercular, nearly as wide as the length of the outer edge—inner lobe very large, rounded internally on the middle of the inner side; tubercular grinders large, rounder on the inner edge, rather wider than the length of the outer edge; the hinder one smaller, but similar to the front one in shape.

Length of the skull 4″ 9‴, of nose 1″ 10‴; width of brain-case 1″ 4½‴, of zygomatic arch 2″ 2½‴.

2. *Nose short, flat, with a central longitudinal groove on the lower surface.*

Tribe 5. Galidiina.

The hind part of the tarsus hairy to the palm; the tail bushy.

10. Galidia.

Galidia, I. Geoff. Compt. Rendus, 1837, p. 580; Mag. de Zool. 1839, pp. 27 & 38, t. 14, 17.

Ears elongate. Body slender. Legs short. Tail elongate, cylindrical, rather larger at the end, ringed? Toes 5—5, arched, webbed; front subequal; the toes and palm bald; the tarsus hairy behind. Claws acute, compressed, retractile. Skull rather ventricose; face short; forehead arched; crown flat. Teeth 36 or 38; false grinders 3/3, 3/3, front very small; flesh-tooth triangular, elongate, longer than broad, and falls early; tubercular grinders 2/1, transverse, the second very small (see skull, *G. elegans*, Geoff. *l. c.* t. 17).

We only possess *Galidia elegans*; and the feet of that species have no relation to those of an *Herpestes*, to which M. I. Geoffroy compares them; they are much more those of a Genet, having short, arched, webbed toes and very acute retractile claws.

* *Tail ringed; "soles of hind feet narrow."* Galidia.

1. Galidia elegans. B.M.

Dark chestnut-brown; tail nearly as long as the body, black-ringed. Length 15 inches; tail 12 inches.

Galidia elegans, I. Geoff. Mag. de Zool. 1839, p. 27, t. 14 & 17; Schinz, Syn. Mamm. i. 378; Gerrard, Cat. Ost. B. M. 76.

Margusta (*Galidia*) *elegans*, Blainv. Ost. t. 9.

Genetta?, A. Smith, S. Afr. Quart. Journ. 52 (see I. Geoff.).

Vounsira, Flacourt, Histoire de Madagascar, p. 154, 1661.

Vausire, Buffon & Daubenton?

Hab. Madagascar (called *Vounsira*).

Skull oblong, rather elongate; forehead shelving, rather convex; the crown flat; the brain-case nearly two-thirds the entire length. False grinders 3/3, the first very small, deciduous, the second and third compressed; the flesh-tooth trigonal, considerably longer than broad at the front edge—the internal tubercle large, and a little behind the front margin. Tubercular grinders—the first subtruncate, oblong, rather wider than long, contracted in the inner side; the second very small, transverse, oblong (see I. Geoff. *l. c.* t. 17).

In the figure cited the brain-cavity is nearly three-fifths the entire length of the skull (that is, measured to the back of the orbits); and the zygomatic arch is rather wider than half the length of the skull.

** *Tail one colour; "soles of hind feet more bald."* Salanoia.

2. Galidia concolor.

Red brown, black-dotted; tail like back, much shorter than the body; ears broad and short. Length 13 inches; tail 7 inches.

Galidia concolor, I. Geoff. Mag. Zool. 1839, p. 30, t. 15; Coquerel, Mag. de Zool. xi. 465; Schinz, Syn. Mamm. i. 377.

G. unicolor, I. Geoff. Compt. Rend. Acad. Sci. 1837, v. 581.

Hab. Madagascar.

3. Galidia olivacea.

Olive-brown, yellow-dotted; tail same colour as the body; false grinders 3/2; tubercular grinders broader than in *G. elegans*, especially the hinder ones.

Galidia olivacea, I. Geoff. Mag. de Zool. 1839, t. 16; Schinz, Syn. Mamm. i. 378.

Hab. Madagascar (*Bernier*) (called "Salano").

? *La petite fouine de Madagascar*, Sganzin in Rev. et Mag. de Zool. 1855, p. 41.

Tribe 6. Hemigalina.

The toes and the middle of the lower part of the tarsus bald; the upper part and sides of lower part hairy. Tail ringed. Fur soft. Frenum hairy. Orbit imperfect.

11. Hemigalea.

Hemigalea (*Hemigalus*), Jourdan, Compt. Rend. 1837; Ann. Sci. Nat. viii. 276, 1837 (not characterized).

Head conical. Nose bald, flat, and with a distinct central groove below; nostrils lateral. Ears moderate, ovate, covered with hair externally. Whiskers numerous, very long, rather rigid, with tufts of slender bristles on the throat, cheeks, and eyebrows. Toes 5—5. Claws acute, semiretractile. Hind feet semiplantigrade; the upper part of the sole hairy, with a narrow bald sole in front below. Frenum covered with hair. Teeth 40; false grinders 3/4, 3/4; tubercular grinders 2/1, 2/1.

The genus is only very indistinctly characterized by M. Jourdan in the papers referred to.

Hemigalea hardwickii. B.M.

Pale yellow; three streaks on the head, two streaks on the nape, some marks on the ears, five crescent-like bands across the back, two rings on the base of the tail, and the end of the tail black.

Viverra hardwickii, Gray, Spic. Zool. ii. 9, t. 1 (not Lesson).

Hylogale zebré, Voyage de la Bonite, t.

Viverra boiéi, S. Müller, Zool. Ind. Arch. t. 18; Schinz, Syn. Mamm. i. 363.

Hemigale zebré, Jourdan, Ann. Sci. Nat. viii. 277.

Paradoxurus derbianus, Gray, Loudon's Mag. N. H. i. (1837) p. 579; Proc. Zool. Soc. 1837, p. 67; De Blainv. Ost. Atlas, t. 7, t. 12 (teeth).

P. ? *zebra*, Gray, Loudon's Mag. N. H. i. (1837) p. 579 (from a drawing).

P. philippensis (partly), Schinz, Syn. Mamm. i. 387.

Hab. Malacca (*Major Farquhar*); Borneo (*Lowe*).

The skull agrees with *Genetta* and *Nandinia* in the hinder opening of the palate being only a short distance behind the line between the back edges of the hinder tubercular grinders. The orbit is very incomplete. The teeth are short, broad, and very unlike those of *Genetta* and *Nandinia*—somewhat similar to those of the genus *Paguma*. The first and second false grinders are compressed, the the third has an inner lobe on the middle of the inner side. The flesh-tooth is triangular, scarcely longer than the width of the middle of the tooth, the large inner lobe occupies nearly the whole inner side. The tubercular grinders are oblong, triangular, much wider than long, rounded on the inner side; the hinder one like the front, but only about half the size. The nose of the skull is elongate. The brain-cavity ovate, ventricose, not suddenly constricted in front. Forehead shelving, rather convex. The bullæ of the ears are oblong, elongate, vesicular, truncated behind, and keeled on the outer edge. Length of the skull 3″ 9‴, of nose 1″ 4½‴, of zygomatic arch and orbit 1″ 6‴; width of brain-case 1″ 3‴, of back of mouth 0″ 1½‴, of zygoma 1″ 10‴.

Tribe 7. ARCTICTIDINA.

The hinder part of the tarsus bald and callous. The tail thick, strong, and prehensile. Fur harsh, bristly. Ears pencilled. Frenum hairy. Orbit of skull imperfect, only defined by a prominence above.

12. ARCTICTIS.

Arctictis, Temm. Monogr. xx. 21, 1820?

Ictides, F. Cuvier; Valenciennes, Ann. des Sci. Nat. iv. 57, 1825; Férus. Bull. Sci. v. 266, 1825.

Head conical. Whiskers numerous, long, rigid, more slender on the cheeks, throat, and eyebrows. Nose acute; underside flat, with a broad central groove. Eyes small. Ears closely covered with long hairs, forming a pencil. Toes 5—5. Claws compressed, acute, retractile. Soles of hind feet broad, entirely bald and callous to the heel. Tail conical, covered with long hair, convolute. Frenum covered with hair? Teeth 36; false grinders 2/3, 2/3; tubercular grinders 2/1, 2/1.

ARCTICTIS BINTURONG. B.M.

Black. Younger with more or less long white tips to the hairs; young, pale dirty yellow.

Viverra ? binturong, Raffles, Linn. Trans. xii. 253.

Arctictis binturong, Temm. Monogr. ii. 308; Fischer, Syn. Mamm. i. 157; Gray, List Mamm. B. M. 54; Gerrard, Cat. Osteol. B. M. 78; Cantor, Cat. Malay. 54; Horsfield, Cat. India House Mus. 94.

A. penicillatus, Temm. Monogr. ii. t. 62; Müller, Zool. Ind. Arch. 32.

Paradoxurus albifrons, F. Cuvier, Mém. Mus. ix. 44, t. 4; Mamm. Lithogr. t.

Ictides, F. Cuv. Dents Mamm. 104, t. 34.

Ictides ater, F. Cuvier, Mamm. Lithogr. t.

I. albifrons, Valenc. Ann. Sci. Nat. iv. 57, t. 1; F. Cuvier, Mém. Mus. ix. t. 4.

Hab. Malacca (*Farquhar*, 1819); Sumatra (*Raffles*); Java (*Temminck*); Tenasserim and Arracan (*Cantor*); Assam, Nepal (*Blyth*).

Varies in the quantity and length of white tips of the hairs.

Major Farquhar says, "It climbs trees, assisted by its prehensile tail, in which it has uncommon strength." M. F. Cuvier (Mém. Mus. ix. 46) doubts this fact; but he is wrong, as any one may see by observing the living animal in the Zoological Gardens.

Skull of young animal elongate. Teeth 36; canines slender; grinders small and far apart; the false grinders, first and second conical, the third compressed; the flesh-tooth small, triangular, inner side rounded; tubercular grinder oblong, trigonal, with a rounded inner edge, larger than the flesh-tooth. Length of skull 4″ 6‴, of nose 1″ 6‴; width of brain-case 1″ 7‴, of zygomatic arch 2″ 4‴.

In the adult skull, false grinders 3/, 3/, compressed, the third triangular; the flesh-tooth triangular, as broad as long, inner edge rounded, with the inner tubercle in the middle; the tubercular grinders small, the first triangular, somewhat like the flesh-tooth, but smaller, the hinder very small, cylindrical (*Temm. Monogr.* ii. t. 50).

The skeleton agrees with *Paradoxurus* in the large number (34) of caudal vertebræ, but differs from it in having a more plantigrade character in the bones of the feet (*Temm. Monogr.* ii. 307).

M. Temminck (Monogr. ii. 308) proposed to arrange *P. aureus* of F. Cuvier with this genus, as it could not be classed with any other group, observing that it is described from a very young specimen not more than one or two months old; and he objects to species being described on such specimens.

Tribe 8. PARADOXURINA.

The hind part of the tarsus bald and callous. The tail cylindrical, hairy, very long, of many vertebræ, revolute. The frenum with a secretory gland. Head elongate. Orbit of skull generally only defined by a slight prominence above. Pupil linear, erect.

This is an exceedingly natural group, well defined by its external characters and general appearance; at the same time the form of the skull and the teeth of the different species present so great an amount of variation that, if one studied the skull only, one would be inclined to distribute them among several different tribes of Carnivora—an instance, among many, which shows the necessity of studying the animal as a whole, and of not devoting one's attention more to the osteological than the external characters, or *vice versâ*.

The gland on the frenum, which is the peculiar character of the genus, was known to Pallas, who called the species *Viverra hermaphrodita* on account of it. It was redescribed and figured by Otto, but overlooked by F. Cuvier when he named the genus from a specimen with a distorted tail!

"M. Temminck observes, "Nom générique donné à tout hasard par F. Cuvier, dont il faut se garder de ne rendre l'application strictement applicable à aucune des espèces de ce groupe."

"La forme et le pouvoir que M. F. Cuvier attribue à cette queue sont basés sur des observations faites sur un sujet soumis à l'état captif, mais ne sont nullement caractérisés pas moins spécifiquement pour son *Pougonne*, notre *Paradoxurus typus*—la Marte des Palmiers du Buffon."—*Mon. Mamm.* ii. 312.

If M. Temminck had observed many of these animals alive, he would have found that many of them have the habit of curling up the end of the tail as it lies on the ground, and that the ends of the tails of those in confinement are often worn away on the side from this habit (see also Bennett, P. Z. S. 1835, p. 118).

M. Temminck describes the claws as "not retractile" (Monogr. ii. p. 312); but Mr. Turner, in his interesting observations on the anatomy of *Paradoxurus typus*, describing the feline habit of the animal, states that the claws are quite as retractile, and scale off at the ends to keep them sharp, as in the Cat; he also says the preputial gland secretes the odorous exhalation (see Proc. Zool. Soc. 1849, p. 24).

"The *Paradoxuri* are in habits like the Civets; their glandular secretion is peculiar, not civet- or musk-like."—*Cantor, Cat.* 32.

Tail very long; caudal vertebræ 36 or 38.

The species of this group have been very imperfectly understood. In the 'Proceedings of the Zoological Society' for 1832 I gave a monograph of the species which the specimens and other materials then available afforded; and I revised the species in the 'Magazine of Natural History' for 1837. The number of species described being so much larger than was then known on the Continent, seems to have excited the distrust of the Continental zoologists as to their distinctness.

M. Temminck, in the second volume of his 'Monographie,' published an essay on the genus, and states that he was indebted to Mr. Ogilby for his assistance. But I fear he must have misunderstood some of Mr. Ogilby's observations; for I can hardly think that an English zoologist, who, from his position as Secretary of the Zoological Society, must have seen many species of the genus alive, could have had such an imperfect acquaintance with the specimens that are to be seen in our menageries.

M. Temminck's 'Monograph' is accurate as far as regards the species which inhabit the Asiatic possessions now or formerly under the Dutch rule. But M. Temminck seems to be entirely unacquainted with the species of continental India and China; he confused, under the same description, species that are very unlike in external characters: some of his figures of the skull do not agree with the skulls of the species which we have extracted from the skins. I may observe that it was formerly the great defect of the osteological collection at Leyden that many of the skeletons had been purchased at sales of private collections in London and elsewhere; so that the accuracy of the determination of the species from which the skulls were obtained solely depended on the accuracy or knowledge of the proprietor, generally more of an anatomist than a zoologist; and as the skin was not kept, there was no means of verifying the name. Hence it is very likely the Nepal *P. grayi* was called in the collection from which it was obtained *P. musanga* of Java. M. Schlegel has been remedying this defect by the preparation of skeletons from well-determined specimens.

M. Jourdan observes, "Ce que nous pouvons dire c'est que dans la collection ostéologique du Muséum il existe des têtes osseuses qui, sous le nom commun de *Paradoxurus typus*, indiquent au moins quatre espèces, et que dans chaqu'une d'elles on peut aisément distinguer un degré tranchant et différent de disposition carnassière."—*Ann. Sci. Nat.* viii. 275, 1837.

The development of the auditory bulla is variable in the genera and species. In *Paguma*, *Paradoxurus*, and *Arctogale* the bulla is large, ventricose, slightly keeled along the lower edge, with a triangular end. In *Nandinia* it is very small, not inflated, and scarcely raised. It varies in form in the different species of *Paradoxurus*, being smallest in *P. bondar*.

The hinder part of the palate of the skull also affords good characters, thus:—

1. The hinder opening of the palate is wide, and nearly in a line with the hinder edge of the last grinder, in *Paradoxurus* and *Nandinia*.

2. The hinder opening of the palate is wide, and further back than the hinder edge of the last grinder, in *Paguma* and *Arctictis*.

3. The hinder opening of the palate is narrow, at the end of a narrow depressed tube, and considerably further back than the hinder edge of the last grinder, in *Arctogale*.

The specimens which are in the British Museum Collection may be divided and arranged thus, from what has been called the "most carnivorous" to the "most omnivorous" form of teeth.

1. The flesh-tooth very narrow, with a small internal process on the front edge. *Nandinia binotata*.
2. The flesh-tooth rather narrow, with a rather small internal lobe on the front edge. *Paradoxurus bondar*.
3. The flesh-tooth rather wider, with a moderate-sized internal lobe on the front edge; teeth moderate. *P. crossii*, *P. nigrifrons*, and *P. zeylanicus*.
4. The flesh-tooth triangular, broad, massive, with a large internal lobe occupying a great part of the inner side.
    - *a.* The teeth elongate, large, massive. *Paradoxurus musanga*, *P. philippensis*, *P. macrodus*, and *Paguma leucomystax*.
    - *b.* The teeth shorter and broader, moderate or small. *Paguma grayi*, *P. larvata*, and *Arctogale trivirgata*.

They may be arranged, according to the form of the adult skull, thus:—

1. The brain-case wide in front, scarcely constricted. Orbit indistinctly marked. Nose broad. *Paguma larvata* and *P. leucomystax*.
2. The brain-case wide in front, and distinctly constricted. Nose rather elongate.

a. Orbit marked only with a short blunt process on the upper hinder edge. *Paguma grayi*.

b. Orbit marked with a rather short, acute, well-marked process on the upper hinder edge. *Nandinia binotata*.

3. The brain-case narrow, and evidently and distinctly constricted in front. The orbit undefined.

a. The face broad; width at the tubercular grinder about four-fifths the length of the palate. *Paradoxurus philippensis, P. crossii, P. nigrifrons, P. fasciatus,* and *P. macrodus*.

b. The face rather elongate; width at the tubercular grinder two-thirds of the length of the palate. *P. zeylanicus, P. bondar,* and *P. hermaphroditus*.

4. The brain-case narrow, suddenly and distinctly constricted in front. The orbit well defined behind. *Arctogale trivirgata*.

The following table may facilitate the determination of the species in the Museum from their external appearance:—

I. *Fur thick, very hairy, rigid, not striped, without any spots under the eyes.* Paguma leucomystax.

II. *Fur very thick, long, with longer rigid hairs, not striped or spotted, but with a spot under the eye.* Paguma grayi, Paradoxurus bondar.

III. *Fur thick, soft, with longer rigid hairs, with a spot under the eye.* Paradoxurus hermaphroditus.

IV. *Fur very thick, close, soft, of nearly uniform length, with a spot under the eyes; cheek whitish, with small dark spots.* Paradoxurus crossii, Paguma larvata, Paradoxurus philippensis, P. nigrifrons, P. musanga, *and* P. dubius (*cheek dark*).

V. *Fur soft; back striped; with no spots under the eyes or on the face.* Arctogale trivirgata.

VI. *Fur soft, thick, close; back spotted; with two yellow spots on the shoulder.* Nandinia binotata.

VII. *Fur very soft, of a uniform colour, with no spot under the eye or on the face.* Paradoxurus zeylanicus.

13. Nandinia, Gray.

Nose conical; underside flat, with a distinct central groove. Frenum covered with hair (?). Nose of skull compressed, produced. The brain-case rather constricted in front behind the orbit. The orbit incomplete, with a well-marked acute process from the forehead, and none from the zygomatic arch behind. The forehead flat, rhombic; produced, angular behind the orbit. Palate wide behind. Teeth 40; false grinders 3/4, 3/4; flesh-tooth elongate, narrow, with a small internal lobe on the front edge; the hinder tubercular very small, circular.

The skull is figured by De Blainville (Ostéogr., Viverra, t. 6) as that of *Paradoxurus? hamiltonii.*

NANDINIA BINOTATA.

Nape with three black parallel streaks, one from the forehead, the other from the ears. Back with numerous black spots. Withers each with a yellow spot. Lips, throat, and beneath rufous grey. Legs grizzled, not spotted. Tail elongate, tapering, with many narrow black rings; end blackish. Length 23 inches; tail 19 inches.

Nandinia binotata, Gray, Cat. Mamm. B. M. 54; Gerrard, Cat. Osteol. B. M. 80.

Viverra binotata, Reinwardt, MS.; Gray, Spic. Zool. 9; Smith, S. African Quart. Journ. ii. 134.

Paradoxurus hamiltonii, Gray, Proc. Zool. Soc. 1832, p. 67; Illust. Ind. Zool. t.; Temm. Monogr. ii. 336, t. 65. f. 1.

Paradoxurus ? binotatus, Gray, P. Z. S. 1832, p. 68.

P. binotatus, Temm. Monogr. ii. 336, t. 65. f. 7–9 (skull); Esq. Zool. 119, 120.

Hab. West Africa: Fernando Po (*Cross*); Ashantee (*Mus. Leyden.*); Guinea (*Mus. Leyden.*).

Varies in the brightness and rufous tint of the fur, and also in the size of the spots; in some they are much larger, and apparently fewer, than in others.

Orbit of skull not defined behind, confluent with the zygomatic cavity. Upper false grinders 3, compressed, first small, third without any distinct inner lobes; flesh-tooth elongate, outer edge considerably longer than the width of the front edge, inner tubercle on the front edge; tubercular grinders two, front triangular, rather wider than the length of the outer edge, hinder small, circular. Length of skull 3″ 4‴, of nose 1″ 1‴; width of brain-case 1″ $2\frac{1}{2}$‴, of zygoma 1″ 10‴.

14. PARADOXURUS.

Paradoxurus, F. Cuv. Mamm. Lithogr. ii. t., 1821.

Platyschista, Otto, Nov. Act. Acad. Leop. xvii. 1090, 1835.

Viverra hermaphrodita, Pallas.

Head conical. Nose flat, and with a central groove beneath. Whiskers numerous, strong, elongate. Toes 5—5. Frenum bald, glandular. The skull with the brain-case strongly and suddenly constricted in front; forehead small, transverse, truncated behind. The orbit very incomplete, with only a short conical prominence above behind, and none on the zygomatic arch below; hinder part of the palate moderate, with only a very slight notch at each side on its front edge. Teeth 40, large; false grinders, $\frac{3-3}{3-2}$; the flesh-tooth triangular or subelongate; the tubercular oblong, transverse.

M. Temminck, in his 'Monographies de Mammalogie,' vol. ii. p. 312 (published in 1855), has given a monograph of this genus; the synonyms are very incorrect.

* *The skull elongate; the nose slender; the width of the head at the last tooth two-thirds the length of the palate; the flesh-tooth elongate, rather narrow, with a small internal lobe on the front edge.* Bondar.

1. Paradoxurus bondar.

Fur very long, hairy, rather rigid, dirty yellowish white varied with the long black tips of the longer and more rigid hairs; end of nose brown, generally with a white central streak. The feet, outer side of fore legs, and end of the tail blackish.

Ichneumon bondar, Buchanan, MS.

Viverra bondar, De Blainville, Journ. de Phys.; Fischer, Syn. Mamm. 172.

Paguma bondar, Horsfield, Cat. Mus. E. Ind. Comp. 68.

Paradoxurus bondar, Gray, P. Z. S. 1832, p. 66; Illust. Ind. Zool. t.; Temm. Esq. Zool. 120; Gerrard, Cat. Osteol. B. M. 79; Schinz, Syn. Mamm. i. 385.

Par. pennantii, Gray, P. Z. S. 1832, p. 66; Illust. Ind. Zool. t.

Par. hirsutus, Hodgson, Asiatic Researches, xix. 72, 1836.

Genetta bondar, Lesson, Mamm. 175.

Hab. Nepal: North Behar and Tarai (*Hodgson*).

This species is easily known from *P. grayi* by the rigid harshness of the fur and the dark colour of the outside of the legs.

Skull narrow, elongate. False grinders distant, the third trigonal; flesh-tooth narrow, elongate, the outer edge longer than the width of the front edge, with the inner lobe on the front margin; tubercular grinder oblong, transverse, rather narrower and rounded on the inner side, wider than long; the hinder tubercular small, oblong, subcircular. Length of skull 4″ 1½‴, of nose 1″ 5‴; width of brain-case 1″ 4½‴, of zygoma 2″ 3‴.

** *The skull moderately broad; the width of the head at the last tooth about four-fifths of the length of the palate; the flesh-tooth rather longer than wide in front, with a moderate-sized internal lobe on the front edge.* Platyschista.

2. Paradoxurus zeylanicus. B.M.

Nearly uniform brown or dark brown; the longer hairs with a bright golden tint; ears nearly naked; whiskers pale brown; tail subcylindrical, sometimes with a single yellow or pale subterminal band; heel of hind feet hairy. Length of body and head 21 inches, tail 17 inches.

Paradoxurus zeylanicus, Gray, Cat. Mamm. B. M. 55 ; Gerrard, Cat. Osteol. B. M. 79 ; Kelaart, Fauna Zeyl.

Viverra zeylanica, Pallas in Schreb. Säugeth. 45 ; Fischer, Syn. Mamm. 172.

V. ceylonensis, Bodd.

? *Paradoxurus aureus*, Desm. Mamm. 540; F. Cuvier, Mém. Mus. ix. 47, t. 4 ; Gerrard, Cat. Osteol. B. M. 79.

P. typicus, De Blainv. Ostéogr. Viverra, t. 12 (teeth), t. 7 (skull).

? *Arctictis aureus*, Fischer, Syn. Mamm. 158.

Hab. Ceylon (*Pallas, Kelaart*).

These animals differ in the intensity of the colour of the fur: some are bright golden, and others much more brown ; the latter is *P. fuscus* of Kelaart. One of our specimens has a bright yellow ring near the tip of the tail.

Third upper false grinders with only a slight indication of a lobe in the middle of the inner edge ; the flesh-tooth with the outer edge scarcely longer than the width of the front edge ; first tubercular large (with the inner edge narrower than the outer one), larger than in *P. philippensis*.

The figure of the skull and of the teeth of the skull named *Paradoxurus typicus* in De Blainville's 'Ostéographie,' tt. 7 & 12, exactly represents the skull and teeth of our *Paradoxurus aureus* received in the skin from Ceylon.

Dr. Kelaart has described, and we have in the British Museum, two varieties of *P. zeylanicus* differing in the intensity of the colour of the fur. In the British Museum we have three skulls, with their permanent teeth, said to have been sent from Ceylon, one being from the skin in the collection sent by Dr. Kelaart: one is larger and rather broader than the other two, which are younger. In two of them the flesh-teeth are nearly similar, with a moderate-sized internal lobe, and the first and hinder upper tubercular grinders are much larger in one of these than in the other. In the third skull, which is the larger, the internal lobe of the flesh-tooth is much longer, compared with the size of the outer portion, than in the preceding skulls; and the first tubercular grinder is much larger, longer, and more massive compared with its width than in either of the preceding; in this skull the hinder tubercular is yet not developed.

Is it that these skulls belong to, and are characteristic of, the two animals which we have thus wrongly called varieties? or does the difference merely arise from their being of two sexes? Genera have been formed on less differences in the Carnivora.

3. PARADOXURUS HERMAPHRODITUS. B.M.

Fur long, rigid, harsh, blackish more or less varied with the pale colours of the lower part of the hairs, scarcely showing three indistinct black streaks on the back ; under fur thick, soft, and very pale reddish ; the feet and end of the tail black ; spot under the eye and the forehead paler, more or less grey or whitish.

Viverra hermaphrodita, Pallas, Schreb. Säugeth. 426.

Paradoxurus hermaphrodita, Gray, P. Z. S. 1832, p. 69.
Platyschista pallasii, Otto, N. Act. Leop. xvii. 1089, t. 71, 72.
Viverra nigra, Desm. Mamm. 208, from Buffon, Suppl. iii. t. 47.
La Marte des Palmiers, ou le Pougonne, F. Cuv. Mamm. Lithogr.
Paradoxurus typus, F. Cuv. Mamm. Lithogr.; Fischer, Syn. Mamm. 158; Temm. Monogr. ii. 215; Esq. Zool. 126; Ogilby, Zool. Journ. iv. 303; Horsfield, Cat. India House Mus. 60; Gerrard, Cat. Osteol. B. M. 80; Schinz, Syn. Mamm. i. 384.
Genette de France, Buffon, H. N. vii. 58; Suppl. iii. t. 47.
Musk or Musky Weasel, Penn. Quadr.
Hab. Continental India, in the plains: Bengal (*Temm.*); Madras (*Jerdon*).

This species differs from the preceding in being small and much blacker. Only one of the wild specimens in the Museum, in a good state of fur, shows any indication of the three black dorsal streaks; but the fur can easily be placed so as to make three more or less interrupted ones apparent: and some of the specimens, which have the tips of the longer hairs worn off, have a somewhat striped appearance on the back; but this is evidently only depending on the bad state of the specimens from their having been kept in confinement.

The skull is very like that of *P. zeylanicus*; the teeth are rather larger; the nose rather narrower in front; the flesh-tooth is rather broad and thick; the front tubercular grinder is transverse, narrower on the inner side, and contracted in front and behind in the middle; the hinder tubercular is very small and circular; the palate-edge is arched behind. The skull is very old, and the orbit is rather more defined behind than usual.

The *Viverra hermaphrodita* of Pallas is thus described:—"Ashy black hairs, grey at the base, black at the tip; beneath pale, a white spot under the eye; ears, throat, and feet black; nose, whiskers, and back with three black streaks; tail longer than the body, black at the tip; claws yellow. Most probably this species is also the *Platyschista pallasii* of Otto; but his figure makes the stripes on the back more distinct than they are usually seen, and the sides of the body too spotted; but it is easy to make a specimen look like the figure.

The figure of the teeth of *P. typus*, in De Blainville's 'Ostéographie,' better represents the teeth of our *P. zeylanicus* than of *P. typus*. Perhaps it is not from the skeleton found on plate 2, which is said to be the animal described by F. Cuvier. The chief difference between the skulls of the two species is, that the internal lobe of the flesh-tooth in *P. zeylanicus* is in a straight line with the front edge of the tooth, whereas in *P. typus* it is rather in front of the outer part of the front edge of the tooth.

The skeleton of the animal first described by F. Cuvier as *Paradoxurus typus* is engraved by De Blainville, Ostéogr. t. 2.

4. Paradoxurus crossii. B.M.

Fur short and close, erect, pale iron-grey without any spots or stripes, spot on side of nose, under orbit, forehead, and base of ears whitish; nose dark brown; feet and ends of the tail black.

Paradoxurus crossii, Gray, Proc. Zool. Soc. ii. 67, 1832; Illust. Ind. Zool. ii. t. 7.

P. musanga, var., Temm. Esq. Zool. 120.

Paguma crossii, Gray, Cat. Mamm. B.M. 54; Gerrard, Cat. Osteol. B. M. 79.

Hab. India (*Brit. Mus.*).

Described from an adult specimen that was confined in the Surrey Zoological Gardens. It is very like *P. grayi*; but the fur is short, thick, and very close, and the colouring of the face is rather different. The nose is brown in the centre, with the brown colour extending under the eyes; the spot under the eye is small and indistinct.

The skulls of the type specimens of *P. crossii* and *P. nigrifrons* in the British Museum are very much alike in general shape, in the breadth of the palate compared with the length, and in the form of the grinders, including the flesh-tooth. Considering the variations which individuals of the same species present, if we had had only the skulls, not knowing the characters of the fur and the colours of the two species, we might have considered them to be varieties of the same species. But knowing that they are the skulls of two very distinct species, one can perceive that the nasal bones are much longer, and the condyles of the skull larger and more oblique, in *P. crossii* than the same parts in the skull of *P. nigrifrons*. The bulla of the ears is differently shaped, ending below in small acute-keeled prominences in *P. crossii*, while in *P. nigrifrons* the whole outer hinder edge is strongly keeled. *P. crossii* is rather narrower at the zygoma. These differences might be peculiar to the individual in each case; and I should not have considered them of specific importance, if I had not known the external characters and appearance of the animals.

The measurements of the two skulls are as follows, in inches and twelfths:—

	P. crossii.	*P. nigrifrons.*
Length of skull	3″ 9‴	3″ 10½‴
—— of nose	1 3	1 3
—— of palate	1 9	1 9
Width of last grinders	1 3½	1 4
—— of brain-case	1 3	1 3
—— of zygoma	2 4½	2 1½

M. Temminck refers *Paradoxurus crossii* to *P. musanga*, and observes that "it is established on the same specimens as served as the model for the figure of Horsfield." How he could have made such an extraordinary mistake I cannot conceive. *P. crossii* was described from a specimen living in the Surrey Zoological Gardens, which did not arrive in this country until several years after Dr. Horsfield's work was published; and Dr. Horsfield's figure was drawn from a stuffed specimen collected by himself in Java, and for years exhibited in the Museum at the India House; while the type specimen of *P. crossii* was, and is still, in the collection of the British Museum. I feel that little reliance can be placed on M. Temminck's statements as to his observations on type specimens. Probably in this case he was misled by misunderstanding some observations of Mr. Ogilby.

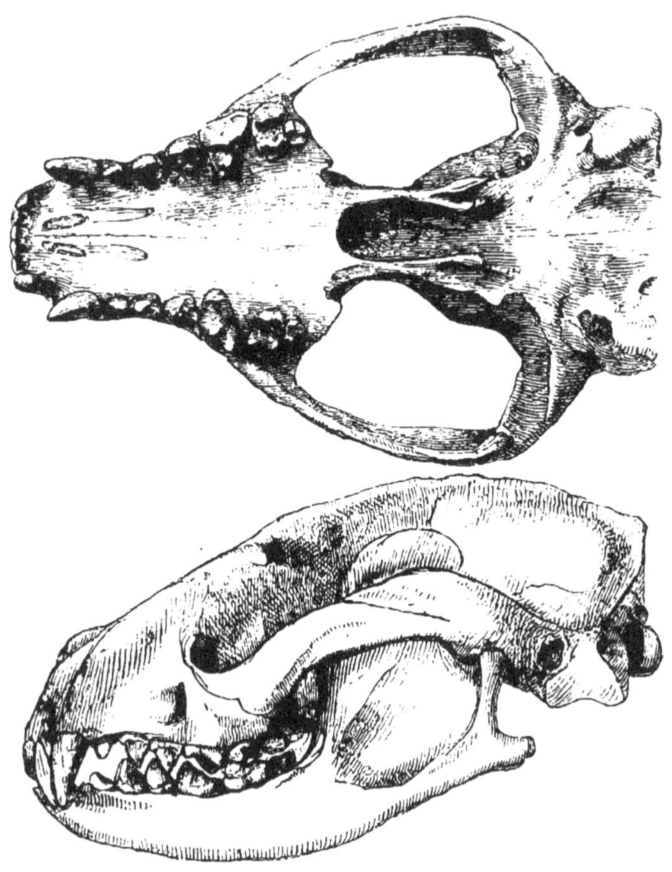

Skull of *Paradoxurus crossii.*

5. Paradoxurus nigrifrons. B.M.

Fur short, close, blackish grey varied with the black tips to the longer hairs; nose, crown, cheeks, and upper part of the throat and feet reddish black; tail-end black; a whitish spot on side of nose, under, and above the eyes; a streak at the base of the ears, and the sides of the throat behind the dark cheeks, whitish.

Paradoxurus nigrifrons, Gray, Cat. Mamm. B. M. 55; Illustr. Ind. Zool. t.; Gerrard, Cat. Osteol. B. M. 79.

Hab. India (*Brit. Mus.*). Single specimen.

The specimen is very like *P. crossii* in the nature and colour of the fur; but it is rather darker in every part, and the crown and cheeks are reddish black, being in *P. crossii* grey or whitish.

In the blackness of the cheeks and throat and the paleness of the forehead this species is allied to *P. musanga*; but the fur is shorter, and I cannot find any indications of dorsal streaks or spots, and the whiteness of the forehead is much more indistinct and diffused than in any specimens of that species I have seen. The specimen has been in confinement; but its fur is in very good condition.

*** *The skull broad; the width of the head at the last tooth about two-thirds of the length of the palate; the flesh-tooth broad, massive, triangular, with a large internal lobe occupying two-thirds of the inner side.* Macrodus.

6. Paradoxurus fasciatus.

Fur short, close, blackish grey; back with five longitudinal black streaks, more or less broken, especially the side ones, into spots; sides, shoulders, and thighs with small spots; face, occiput, chin, throat, and end of tail black; forehead, spot on side of nose, and under orbit white.

Viverra fasciata, Desm. Mamm. 209.

Genetta fasciata, Lesson, Mamm. 174.

V. geoffroyii, Fischer, Syn. Mamm. 171.

Paradoxurus musanga, Gray, P. Z. S. 1832, p. 16.

P. musanga, var. *javanica*, Horsf. Java, t.; Temm. Monogr. ii. 317, t. 53. f. 2–5, t. 54. f. 1, 2, 3 (skulls); Esquis. Zool. 120; Horsf. Cat. India House Mus. 62; Gerrard, Cat. Osteol. B. M. 80; Schinz, Syn. Mamm. i. 382.

Viverra musanga, Raffles, Linn. Trans. xiii. 255.

Musang, Marsden, Sumatra, 110, t. 12.

Paradoxurus typus, var. *sumatranus*, Fischer, Syn. Mamm. 159.

P. setosus, Homb. & Jacq. Voy. de l'Astr. Zool. iii. 25, t.

Var. Forehead more white:—

? *Paradoxurus pallasii*, Gray, P. Z. S. 1832, p. 67; Illust. Ind. Zool. t.; Horsfield, Cat. India House Mus. 63.

? *P. albifrons*, Bennett, in Zool. Gardens List (not of Cuvier).

Var. Tip of tail white.

Hab. Malacca, Java, Sumatra, Borneo (*Horsfield*).

M. Temminck confounds *Paradoxurus crossii* and *P. pallasii* with this species (see Esquis. Zool. 220).

The size of the spots on the face and the extent and pureness of the white on the forehead vary; but the animal always has a distinct brown or black mark on the back of the cheeks, most distinctly defined on the lower part of the face. The species has been divided into several on account of these differences.

A specimen from Borneo in the Museum is so black that the spots are scarcely to be distinguished; but there are specimens in the collection that are intermediate between it and those which have the common colour of the species.

The skull is like that of *P. nigrifrons*; the teeth are much more thick and massive; the flesh-tooth broader, and with a much larger internal lobe; the first tubercular is more square, nearly as wide on the inner as on the outer side; the hinder tubercular is small, subcircular; the palate has an angular notch behind; the zygomatic arch is also a little wider.

The length of the skull 4″, of the nose 1″ 4‴, of palate 1″ 10½‴; width at tubercular grinder 1″ 6‴, at zygoma 2″ 3‴, of brain-case 1″ 5‴.

Paradoxurus quinquelineatus and *Paradoxurus musangoides*, Gray, Loudon's Mag. N. H. i. 579, 1837, are perhaps only varieties of the young animal of this species.

Viverra fasciata, Desm. Mamm. 209 (not of Gmelin), described as pale yellow, with longitudinal series of brown spots, end of the nose and frontal cross band white, is also probably the same. It cannot be *Viverricula madagascariensis*, as the forehead is not particularly white. This is perhaps the *Platyschista* ——? which Otto notices in 'Nova Acta Acad. Leop. Carol.' xvii. 1102.

Hab. Java? (*Mus. Paris.*).

7. Paradoxurus dubius. B. M., type.

Pale yellowish ashy brown, with three indistinct, rather interrupted, darker bands and some indistinct darker spots on the sides; head, ears, and feet chestnut; forehead with an indistinct whitish band; spot on side of nose and under eyes white.

Paradoxurus dubius, Gray, P. Z. S. 1832, p. 66; Cat. M.B.M. 56.

Hab. Java (*Brit. Mus.*).

The skull is in the skin; so I have not been able to examine it. This species may be only a very pale variety of *P. fasciatus*.

8. Paradoxurus philippensis. B.M., type.

Fur blackish, with a silvery gloss; spot under eyes distinct; cheeks dark brown; head, feet, and the greater part of the tail blacker; the back with three indistinct narrow black streaks, which converge near the rump, and with a series of very indistinct small ones on the upper part of the sides; sides of forehead, chest, and beneath whiter; whiskers white and black; ears hairy.

Var. Dorsal stripes none. B.M.

Var. Albino, yellowish white. B.M.

P. aureus, Waterhouse, Cat. Zool. Soc.

Martes philippensis, Camellus, Phil. Trans. xxv. 2204.

Paradoxurus zeylanicus (partly), Gray, Cat. Mamm. B. M. 55.

P. philippensis, Temm. Monogr. ii., Esq. Z. 120 (not Jourdan).

Hab. Manilla, Philippines: Casmiguind (*Cuming*).

The colours vary much in intensity, and in the lighter and darker specimens the spots and streaks are scarcely visible; the white on the side of the forehead in front of the base of the ears also varies in distinctness and extent; the spot under the eyes is generally distinct. This species is like *P. nigrifrons* and *P. musanga* in many respects; but it differs from them both in the crown of the head being paler like the back, and from *P. nigrifrons* in having three dorsal stripes; but in one specimen, from the Philippines, these stripes are quite invisible; yet in every other respect this is like the other specimens, and it differs from the specimen of *P. nigrifrons* in the colour of the crown.

Third upper false grinder with a well-marked linear tubercle on the hinder inner edge; the flesh-tooth tubercular, the outer edge not longer than the width of the front margin; front tubercular tooth oblong, the inner and outer edge of about the same width, smaller than in *P. zeylanicus*.

9. PARADOXURUS MACRODUS. B.M., type.

The skull with a rather elongated nose; the third upper false

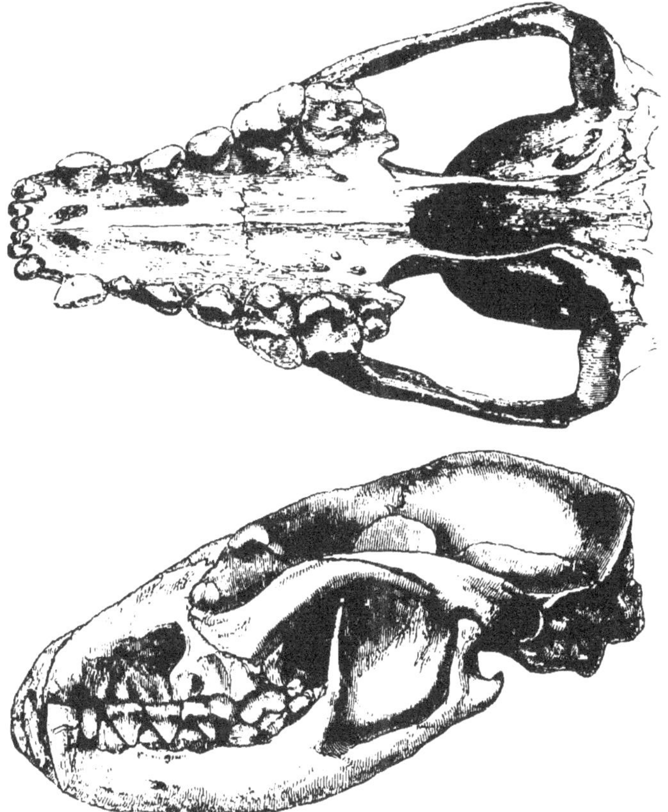

Skull of *Paradoxurus macrodus*.

grinder has a well-marked cingillum and a rudimentary lobe on the inner side. The flesh-tooth is very massive, with four large and two small cones; the inner lobe occupies more than half the inner part of the tooth, with two unequal cones, the front one being nearly as large as the middle one on the outer side. The front tubercular very large, oblong, with nearly equal sides and large tubercles; the hinder upper tubercular much smaller, circular.

Length of skull 4″ 4‴, of nose 1″ 6‴; width of brain-case 1″ 5‴, of zygoma 2″ 3‴.

Hab. ——?

This skull was received from the Museum of the Zoological Society; it was marked in the catalogue, "Skull of a Genet undetermined."

15. Paguma.

Paguma, Gray, Zool. Misc. 9, 1831; Proc. Zool. Soc. i. 95, 1831; ii. 65, 1832.

? *Amblyodon*, Jourdan, Compt. Rend. 1837.

Nose flat beneath, with a central longitudinal groove. The skull broad, short. Brain-case broad between the orbits, only moderately constricted in front; forehead triangular behind, extending beyond the back edge of the orbits. The orbit very incomplete, with a very short acute prominence above behind, and none on the zygomatic arch below; hinder part of palate broad, with a very slight notch on each side of its front edge; the front of the palate broad, about as wide as three-fourths of its length. Teeth small or moderate; flesh-tooth triangular, the front edge about as broad as long on the outer edge; the front tubercular oblong, inner edge shorter, rounded.

The skull of this genus is easily known by the distinct forehead, the edge of the temporal muscles even in the oldest specimen leaving a plane triangular space over the back of the eyes.

This genus was first established on an animal that had not completely shed its teeth; but the examination of the adult skull has justified the separation.

The following are the most prominent peculiarities of the skulls of the three species:—

1. *P. larvata* is the smallest, has the broadest nose, as shown by the shape of the roof of the mouth or palate, and the smallest teeth.
2. *P. grayi* is next in size, has a longer and narrower nose, larger teeth, and a larger and more convex forehead.
3. *P. leucomystax* is the largest, with a short, very broad nose, and wide palate, and very large massive teeth.

The hinder opening of the palate in *P. larvata* and *P. leucomystax* is angularly cut out behind; in *P. grayi*, arched out. The brain-case is widest and least contracted in front in *P. larvata* and *P. leucomystax*, and most so in *P. grayi*. This contraction becomes more decided as the specimens increase in age.

* *Skull short; brain-case scarcely constricted in front; the nose very broad.* Paguma.

1. Paguma larvata. B.M., type.

Fur grey brown; head, neck, whiskers, feet, and end of the tail black; chest, streak up the face and forehead, and spots above and beneath the eyes whitish grey.

Paguma larvata, Gray, P. Z. S. 1830, p. 95; 1831, p. 65; Gerrard, Cat. Osteol. B. M. 79.

Gulo larvatus, Temm.; H. Smith, Griffith's A. K. ii. 281, t.

Viverra larvata, Gray, Spic. Zool. 9.

Paradoxurus larvatus, Gray, P. Z. S. 1832, p. 67; Illust. Ind. Zool. t.; Temm. Monogr. ii. t. 65. f. 1–3, t. 55. f. 1–3 (skull); Esq. Zool. 120; Schinz, Syn. Mamm. i. 384.

Hab. China (*J. Reeves*, 1827); Formosa (*Swinhoe*).

M. Temminck has confused *Paradoxurus grayi*, *P. nipalensis*, and *P. laniger* with this species, and gives Himalaya and Thibet as the habitat (see Esq. Zool. 126).

Flesh-tooth oblong, trigonal, rounded at the corners, about as wide as the length of the outer edge; the inner lobe occupying nearly the whole of the inner side, rounded internally. The soles are bald nearly to the heel. The hair is dull grey brown, with a black ring and whitish tips; the hairs of the blacker part are black nearly to the base; the white on the chest is spread out laterally on the front of the shoulder.

M. Temminck, after giving the proper synonyms of this species, continues, "M. Ogilby indique encore *Paradoxurus laniger*, Hodgson, et *P. grayi*, Bennet" (Proc. Zool. Soc. for 1836, p. 118); and adds, "Patrie: M. Ogilby, qui a vu à Londres une douzaine d'individus de cette espèce, me dit qu'elle vient du continent de l'Inde. Elle vit dans toute la chaîne basse des monts Himalaya. Le plus grand nombre vient du Népaul. Il est probable que le sujet du musée dans les Pays-Bas vient aussi de cette contrée, ayant été acquis à Londres."—*Mon. Mamm.* ii. 331.

The whole of these observations of Mr. Ogilby refer to a species quite distinct (indeed having no relation to *P. larvata*), which does inhabit Nepaul, while *P. larvata* has not hitherto been received from anywhere but China, and appears to be the species of that country. It is the less excusable that M. Temminck should have made such a comparison, when the true habitat is given in the description of the animal in the 'Proceedings of the Zoological Society,' which he quotes, and I have never yet seen the *P. larvata* alive in this country.

2. PAGUMA LEUCOMYSTAX. B.M., type.

Black brown with elongated black shining hairs; orbits dark brown; face pale, without any orbital spots, a large spot at the lower angle of the ear; tip of the tail black (rarely white); whiskers rigid, white; ears large and rounded, not bearded.

Paguma leucomystax, Gray, Cat. Mam. B. M. 55; Gerrard, Cat. Osteol. B. M. 79.

Paradoxurus leucomystax, Gray, Loud. Mag. N. H. 1837; S. Müller, Verh. i. 55; Temm. Monogr. ii. 325, t. 64. f. 4–6 (skull); Schinz, Syn. Mamm. i. 383.

Var. 1. Tip of tail white; white on face more extended:—

Paradoxurus jourdanii, Gray, Loudon's Mag. N. H. i. 579, 1837, from Mus. Leyden.

P. ogilbii, Fraser, Zool. Typica, t.; Temm. Esq. Zool. 120.

P. leucocephalus, Gray, Voy. Samarang. (B.M.)

P. philippensis (partly), Schinz, Syn. 387.

Var. 2. Albino.

Hab. Sumatra and Borneo (*Mus. Leyden.*).

The lower and longest whiskers are white, and the upper ones (which are placed just above them) are black and more slender.

The half-grown specimen, which I described as *Paradoxurus leucocephalus*, appears, on recomparison with the series of specimens, to be only a specimen with more white on the head than usual. The fur is in a bad state, the animal having been kept in confinement. The tip of the tail is white, as in the *P. ogilbii* of Fraser, which agrees with it in the whiteness of the head.

** *Skull rather longer; brain-case slightly constricted in front; nose rather elongate, narrower; teeth small.* Amblyodon.

3. Paguma grayi (type), Bennett & Hodgson. B.M.

Fur long and rigid, rather woolly, iron-grey, beneath paler; base of ears and sides of nose browner; tail elongate, flat at the base.

Paguma grayi, Gray, Cat. Mamm. B. M. 54; Cat. Hodgson Coll. 9; Gerrard, Cat. Osteol. Brit. Mus. 78; Horsfield, Cat. India House Mus. 66.

Paradoxurus grayi, Bennett, P. Z. S. 1835, p. 18.

P. larvatus, var., Temm. Esq. Zool. 120 (!).

P. bondar, Temm. Monog. ii. 332, t. 55. f. 1–4 (skull, not syn.).

? *P. leucopus*, Ogilby, Zool. Journ. iv. 303, ? var.

P. nipalensis, Hodgson, Asiatic Research. Bengal, xix. 76, 1836; Schinz, Syn. Mamm. i. 387.

Amblyodon doré, Jourdan, Ann. Sci. Nat. viii. 276, 1837.

Paradoxurus auratus, De Blainville, Ostéographie (Viverra), t. 12 (teeth).

Hab. India: Nepal.

The spot on the side of the face, under the eye, is sometimes very indistinct. The blackish ends of the hairs of the back, when crowded together at the crease of the neck, and when brushed towards the middle of the back, give the appearance of a dark band or streak; but there is no real band or streak in this species.

Skull swollen. False grinders moderate, rather compressed, conical, blunt, without any internal process; the flesh-tooth triangular, rather longer on the outer edge than the width of the front edge; the internal tubercles triangular, rather behind the front edge, inner side rather angular; tubercular grinders oblong, transverse, about as wide as the length of the outer edge, inner side narrower and rounded; hinder tubercular very small, circular.

Length of skull 4″ $6\frac{1}{2}$‴, of nose 1″ $5\frac{1}{2}$‴; width of brain-case 1″ 6‴, of zygoma 2″ 6‴.

This skull is much more ventricose, and the head is much shorter and broader, than in *P. bondar*.

Paradoxurus leucopus, Ogilby, Zool. Journ. iv. 300, t. 35, 1829, Temm. Esq. Zool. 120, "band round the loins, the feet, and the tip of the tail pure white," is probably, from the description, an accidental variety of the *P. grayi*. The specimen does not appear to have been preserved.

I believe the specimen which I described in 1837, under the name of *P. jourdanii*, 'Mag. of Nat. Hist.' i. 579, from a specimen which M. Jourdan purchased in London for the Lyons Museum, is the same as the one here described.

The only character that M. Jourdan gives is the following:— "Cette à laquelle il a donné le nom d'*Amblyodon doré* est celle qui offre la disposition dentaire la plus omnivore, celle qui, par conséquent, rappelle le mieux ce qui a lieu dans les *Rasores*, chez lesquels les deux bords dentaires sont presque égaux en hauteur et en épaisseur, également tuberculeux, et ont les deux arrières molaires approchant le plus d'être égales et semblables dans leurs côtés interne et externe."

"L'*Amblyodon* a un pelage fort grossier, rude, assez long et presque unicolore, seulement plus foncé en dessus, autour des yeux, avec les extrémités noires en dessus, comme la *Mustela*."—*Ann. Sci. Nat.* viii. 276, 1837.

This character suits more than one Indian species; but fortunately M. de Blainville, in his valuable 'Ostéographie,' has figured a skull under the name of *Paradoxurus auratus*, which is probably the one named by M. Jourdan, and certainly is the same as the *Paradoxurus grayi* of Mr. Bennett. It may be observed that M. Jourdan was in England shortly after I had described the species in the 'Magazine of Natural History': he saw my specimens, and even referred to my paper in his 'Mémoire' (p. 275); but he redescribed my *Paradoxurus derbianus* as *Hemigale zebra*, and *P. jourdanii* as *Amblyodon doré*, without reference to their synonyms, though the latter is from the same specimen, I believe, as I described with his permission.

Paradoxurus laniger, Hodgson, MS. (*Paguma laniger*, Gray, Cat. Mamm. B. M. 55).

P. larvatus, var., Temm. Esq. Zool. 120 (!); Monogr. ii.

Hab. Nepal (*Hodgson*).

This species is only known from a skin without any skull, and in a very bad state.

16. Arctogale.

Arctogale, Peters, Handb. für Zool. 98 (ined.).

Head conical. Nose compressed, flat, and with a central groove beneath. Whiskers slender, very long, brown. Ears rounded, covered with short hair. Toes 5—5; claws short, retractile. Soles of hind feet broad, bald nearly to the heel. Tail elongate, slender, subcylindrical. The frenum covered with hair. Teeth 40.

Skull elongate. Nose produced. Brain-case rather wide, but constricted and subcylindrical in front. Forehead broad, angular behind, and extending beyond the back edge of the orbits. The orbits nearly complete behind, there being an elongated slender process from the side of the forehead and a well-marked angle on the upper edge of the zygomatic arch. Hinder part of the palate very narrow, with a deep notch on each side in front, on a level with the hinder tubercular; front of palate as wide as two-thirds its length. Teeth small; the flesh-tooth triangular, with a long, narrow internal lobe; tubercular grinders oblong, the first nearly as long as broad.

"I have formed this into a genus, on account of the smallness of the teeth and the protraction of the palate."—*Peters's Letter*, Nov. 11, 1864.

I had already distinguished the genus, but gladly adopt Dr. Peters's unpublished name to prevent the useless increase of generic names.

ARCTOGALE TRIVIRGATA. B.M., type.

Blackish brown, slightly silvered with the pale tips to the hairs; back with three narrow black streaks; throat, chest, and undersides dirty white; the head and tail black; feet blackish brown.

Paguma trivirgata, Gray, Cat. Mamm. B. M. 55; Gerrard, Cat. Osteol. B. M. 79; Temm. Monogr. ii. 335, t. 53. f. 1 (skeleton); Horsfield, Cat. India House Mus. 64.

Viverra trivirgata, Reinhardt, in Mus. Leyden.

Paradoxurus trivirgatus, Gray, P. Z. S. 1832, p. 67; Temm. Esq. Zool. 120.

P. lævidens, fide Parzudaki's MS.

Hab. Java and Sumatra (*Temm.*); Malacca (*Finlayson*); Tenasserim (*Blyth*).

The black streak varies in distinctness and length in the different specimens, being sometimes very black and extending from the back of the head to the base of the tail, in others only distinctly visible in the middle of the back. The head and end of the tail are always blacker, and the throat whitish. There is no white spot under or above the eye; so that it cannot be *Viverra hermaphrodita* of Pallas, which is described as having three dorsal streaks; and I cannot observe any baldness of the frenum in the stuffed specimens. The tail in some lights looks as if it were very obscurely marked with narrow blackish rings; but they are not distinctly defined in any light.

The Museum procured a young specimen from M. Parzudaki, of Paris, under the name of "*P. lævidens*, inter *P. larvatum* et *P. grayi* intermedius, Ceylon." The habitat and the affinities are mistakes.

Species of this group requiring further examination.

PARADOXURUS STIGMATICUS, Temm. Esq. Zool. 120.

Fur short and smooth; that of the nape, upper part of the body, the sides, the four members, and the tail is red-brown, with a silvery lustre; the silky hairs of all parts are tipped with yellowish white. Head black brown, with a fulvous lustre; a pure-white longitudinal band extends from the forehead to the origin of the muffle, covering the ridge of the nose; the ears naked externally, with the base of the inner side hairy. The tail and the end of the tail chocolate.

Length of head and body 17 inches, tail 19 inches.

Hab. Borneo (*Schwaner, Temm., Mus. Leyden.*).

A single, very old, male specimen. Size and form of *P. trivirgatus.*

PARADOXURUS LEUCOTIS, Blyth, in Horsf. Cat. India House Mus. 66.

Fur rather long, soft, silky; of upper part of the body, neck, head, and two-thirds of the tail tawny, becoming reddish brown on the back and sides; thighs and legs, throat and abdomen, lighter; tail very long, and deep chestnut-brown; whiskers long, blackish brown; nose with a central white line; ears scarcely covered with scattered yellowish hairs.

Hab. Tenasserim, Arracan (*Mus. India*).

PARADOXURUS STRICTUS.

Paradoxurus strictus, Hodgson, Ann. & Mag. Nat. Hist. 1855, xvi. 105.

General colour grey, with a slight rusty shade; two prominent white spots on each side of the head, one beneath the eye oblong, tending forward, one behind the eye larger, triangular, tending backward; five continuous stripes, regularly defined and straight, of a deep black colour, commencing on the neck, extend over the whole length of the body, having on each side beneath an interrupted band of black spots. Abdomen grey. Tail exceeding the body in length; mixed grey and black at the base; the terminal portion black, the colour increasing in deepness towards the extremity. Legs black. Throat grey, with a medial black stripe. Ears developed.

Length from the snout to the root of the tail 23 inches, of the tail 25 inches.

Hab. India.

PARADOXURUS QUADRISCRIPTUS.

Paradoxurus quadriscriptus, Hodgson, Ann. & Mag. Nat. Hist. 1855, xvi. 106; Gray, P. Z. S. 1853, p. 191.

General colour grey, with a slight rufous shade extending over the whole of the body, over one-half of the tail, over the forehead and the lower part of the ear. On the back and parts adjoining, four well-defined continuous black stripes pass from the neck to the rump, having a shorter interrupted band on each side. The bridge of the nose in the middle, a well-defined narrow streak from the canthus of the eye, the neck, the feet, and the terminal part of the tail are black; on the upper part of the neck the hairy covering is slightly variegated black and grey, the separate piles being grey at the base and black at the tip. The fur is soft, lengthened, and straggling.

The entire length of this species is 50 inches, 26 of which are occupied by the head and body, and 24 by the tail.

I could not discover any external differences between the specimens which Mr. Hodgson sent, under the name of *P. quadriscriptus*, from Nepal, and *P. musanga* (see Proc. Zool. Soc. 1853, p. 191). The skull has not been compared.

PARADOXURUS PREHENSILIS, Gray, P. Z. S. 1832, ii. 66; Illust. Ind. Zool.; Horsf. Cat. India House Mus. 63; Temm. Esq. Zool. 120.

Ichneumon prehensilis, Hamilton, MS. India House.

Viverra prehensilis, De Blainv. in Desm. Mamm. 208.

Hab. India.

The species, which has only been described from Dr. Buchanan Hamilton's drawing, copied in my 'Indian Zoology,' has not yet occurred to me. M. Temminck, who never could have seen it, states it to be "a constant variety" of *Paradoxurus musanga* (Esq. Zool. 120); but, as far as I know, *P. musanga* is confined to the Malay Islands.

PARADOXURUS FINLAYSONII, Gray, P. Z. S. 1832, p. 68, from Mr. Finlayson's drawing in Library of E. India Company; Horsfield, Cat. India House Mus. 65.

Hab. Malacca (*Finlayson's drawing*).

Probably the same as *P. musanga*.

PARADOXURUS CRASSICEPS, Pucheran, Rev. et Mag. Zool. vii. 392; Arch. für Naturg. 1856, p. 43.

PARADOXURUS ANNULATUS, Wagner, in Schreber's Säugeth. Suppl. ii. 253; Schinz, Syn. Mamm. i. 386.

P. *supra niger fulvo mixtus, subtus ferrugineus, lutescens; cauda nigro annulata, auriculis dense pilosis.*

Hab. ——? (*Mus. Munich*).

Tribe 9. CRYPTOPROCTINA.

The hinder part of the tarsus bald and callous; the tail long, covered with long flaccid hair; the head short, subglobose; the orbit of the skull incomplete behind.

17. CRYPTOPROCTA.

Cryptoprocta, Bennett, P. Z. S. 1832, p. 46; Trans. Zool. Soc. i. 137.

Head conical. Whiskers rigid, very long. Ears large, covered with short hair externally. Nose with a distinct, naked, central longitudinal groove below. Tail elongate, covered with long flaccid hair. Soles of feet naked. Toes united by a web.

CRYPTOPROCTA FEROX. B.M.

Fur pale brown; hair short, uniform, that of the back with a small pale tip; under fur dusky.

Cryptoprocta ferox, Bennett, P. Z. S. 1833, p. 46; Trans. Zool. Soc. i. 137, t. 14; Gerrard, Cat. Ost. B. M. 81; De Blainv. Ost. Atlas, 15, 96, t. 6 & 12; Schinz, Syn. Mamm. i. 381.

C. typicus, A. Smith, S. African Quart. Journ. ii. 134.

Hab. Madagascar (*Charles Telfair*).

The skull of the *Cryptoprocta*, with its milk-teeth, is ovate, with a very short, rather compressed nose, large orbit, imperfect behind, and very short, much turned-out, slender zygomatic arches. The teeth are somewhat like those of a *Viverra malaccensis* of the same age; but the face is much shorter, and the palate broader in front, and the flesh-tooth more compressed longitudinally. The false grinders 2/3; the upper front are small and much worn. The flesh-tooth is long, compressed, with slight processes, without any tubercle on the middle of the inner side. The tubercular is triangular; the front edge rather the longer; the outer edges oblique, and inner one narrow, rounded, with three slightly raised tubercles on the front, and one on the hinder part of the crown.

Length of the skull 3 inches; width of brain-case, over ears, $1\frac{1}{3}$ inch, at zygomatic arch $1\frac{2}{3}$ inch.

The *Cryptoprocta* "has an anal pouch, and when violently enraged it emits a most disagreeable smell, very like that of *Mephites*; when at liberty, it lies constantly in a rolling position, sleeping always on its side or even on its back, holding with its fore feet the small wires of its cage."

See M. J. Geoffroy's observations on this genus (Mag. Zool. 1839, p. 25). He says it is very different from *Galidia*—which no one could doubt, if he studied the description of the feet:—

"Le *Cryptoprocta* de Bennett, peutêtre le même que l'*Eupleres* de M. Doyer, semble plutôt être le représentant des *Paradoxures* de Madagascar."—*Jourdan, Ann. Sci. Nat.* viii. 272, 1837. This is a mistake, as any one may prove, by comparing the skulls, which are both figured in De Blainville's 'Ostéographie.' M. Pucheran also appears to think that this animal and the one described as *Eupleres goudotii* may not be different (see Rev. et Mag. Zool. 1858, p. 40).

II. THE DOG-FOOTED VIVERRIDÆ (*Cynopoda*).

The hind feet slender; underside bald, or more or less covered with scattered hairs. The toes slender, free, compressed, straight, slightly hairy; the claws exserted, exposed, blunt at the end. The orbit of the skull complete, or only slightly imperfect on the hinder edge. The body elongate; legs generally short. The fur is generally harsh, grizzled. The back is not crested. The tail conical or cylindrical, hairy, not dark-ringed. The anal pouches shallow, or not present.

A. *The nose short; underside flat, with a central longitudinal furrow.* Herpestcacea.

Tribe 10. Herpestina.

Head elongate, conical; tail conical or cylindrical; back streaked; claws elongate, compressed.

18. Galidictis.

Galidictis, I. Geoff. Compt. Rend. 1837, p. 580; Mag. Zool. 1839, t. 18; Schinz, Syn. Mamm. i. 360; Gray, P. Z. S. 1848, p. 21 (not Hodgson).

Galictis, I. Geoff. Compt. Rend. 1837, p. 581.

Nose flat, and with a groove below. Ears moderate. Tail bushy. Whiskers slender. Toes 5—5; front claws elongate, compressed, much arched; thumb low down, with a long claw. Hinder toes:—third and fourth longest, subequal; great toes low down; claws all moderate, compressed. Soles broad, bald the whole width to the heel. False grinders 3/3. Tail subcylindrical, curved, with long hairs. Back streaked.

1. Galidictis vittata. B.M.

Galidictis vittata, Gray, P. Z. S. 1848, p. 21, pl. 1; in Zool. Sulphur, t.; Coquerel, Mag. de Zool. xi. 465, t. 18. f. 2.

Grey, black-and-white grizzled; back and sides with eight nearly equal, parallel, narrow, black-brown streaks; chin and beneath pale brown; hind feet and outer sides of fore legs reddish brown; tail subcylindrical, bushy, black-and-grey grizzled, white towards the end; hairs elongate, brownish white, with two, rarely three, broad black rings.

Hab. Madagascar (*T. Thompson*) (*Mus. Brit.*).

The skull described in the Proc. Zool. Soc. is not quite adult; it has a small adult false molar.

2. Galidictis striata.

Pale brown; seven or nine longitudinal black streaks, the middle one on each side behind short; head and limbs pale brown; tail whitish.

Galidictis striata, I. Geoff. Mag. de Zool. 1839, t. 18, 19; Schinz, Syn. Mamm. i. 360; Gerrard, Cat. Ost. B. M. 76.

Galictis striata, I. Geoff. Compt. Rend. Acad. Sci. 1837, p. 581.

Mustela striata, Geoff. Mus. Paris.; Fischer, Syn. Mamm. 224.

Pictorius striatus, Cuvier, Règne An. ed. 2, p. 144.

La Belette grise de Madagascar, Sganzin, Rev. et Mag. Zool. 1855, 41.

Hab. Madagascar.

In the figure the brain-cavity is nearly three-fifths the entire length of the skull; and the skull at the widest part of the zygomatic arch is as large as the brain-cavity. Skull oblong, rather elongate; brain-cavity rather more than half the entire length; orbit very incomplete behind; forehead arched; crown flat; upper false grinders two, compressed; the flesh-tooth elongate, trigonal, much longer than broad at the front edge—the internal tubercle moderate, on the front edge; tubercular grinders transverse, the first rather trigonal, narrow on the inner side, the second oblong, much smaller (see I. Geoff. *l. c.* t. 19).

b. *Back grizzled; claws short, curved.*

19. HERPESTES.

Herpestes, Illiger.
Mangusta, Olivier.
Ichneumon, Geoff.

Body elongate; limbs moderate; back grizzled. Tail conical, covered with long hairs. Toes 5—5; claws short, compressed. Pupil linear, erect. Skull elongate. Teeth 40; false grinders $\frac{3-3}{4-4}$; flesh-tooth elongate, narrow, longer than broad on the front edge; tubercular grinders transverse.

* *Animal large; hair of body and tail long, harsh; tail ending in a black pencil.*

1. HERPESTES ICHNEUMON. B.M.

Grey, hairs largely ringed; head and middle of the back darker; legs reddish; feet and end of tail black, with a long flaccid pencil; under fur short, reddish.

Herpestes ichneumon, Gray, Cat. Mamm. B. M. 51; Gerrard, Cat. Ost. B. M. 73.
Viverra ichneumon, Linn. S. N.
Herpestes pharaonis, A. Smith, S. A. Quart. Journ. i. 49; Schinz, Syn. Mamm. i. 367.
Ichneumon pharaonis, Geoff. Mém. Egypt.
Mangusta ichneumon, Fischer, Syn. 163.
Ichneumon ægypti, Tiedem. Zool. i. 364.
Mangouste d'Egypte, F. Cuv. Mamm. Lith. t.
Mangouste d'Alger, F. Cuv. Mamm. Lith. t.
Hab. North Africa: Egypt; Senegal (*Reade, B. M.*); Cape Filpila, 1850.

The skull is elongate, rather slender; the brain-case (that is, from the occiput to the back edge of the orbit) is three-fifths of the entire length; the crown is straight; the forehead arched and rather convex; the orbits are not quite complete behind. The teeth are normal, moderate-sized; the flesh-grinders of the upper jaw rather narrow, the front being two-thirds the length of the outer edge; the front tubercular trigonal, transverse; the hinder one small and oblong, transverse. Length $3\frac{8}{12}$ inches, width at zygomatic arch 2 inches—the same as the length of the brain-case; width of brain-case $1\frac{5}{8}$ inch. The skull is contracted in front, just over the back edge of the orbits. Lower jaw very shelving in front; false grinders 4/4; tubercular grinder oblong, elongate, moderate, with a very obscure anterior lobe, two lateral and one larger hinder lobe.

2. HERPESTES CAFFER. B.M.

Like the preceding, but darker; under fur shorter, red; end of tail with a long, black, flaccid pencil.

Herpestes caffer, Licht. Verz. der Säugeth. 1835; Wagner, Gel. Anz. ix.; Gray, Cat. Mamm. B. M. 51; Gerrard, Cat. Ost. B. M. 73; Schinz, Syn. Mamm. i. 368; A. Smith, S. A. Q. J. 50.

Viverra caffra, Gmelin, S. N.

Ichneumon pharaonis, Verreaux.

Hab. S. Africa, on plains away from the sea; Natal (*Kraus*).

The skull of *H. caffer* is elongate, larger and longer than that of the adult *H. ichneumon*, and is more convex on the forehead and behind the orbit. The front of the brain-case is contracted some distance behind the back edge of the orbit, while in *H. ichneumon* this contraction is just over that part. The zygomatic arch is very long, much longer than in *H. ichneumon*, and not so arched out as it is in the latter species. Like as the two species are externally, they are very distinct in the form of their skulls. The teeth of the two species are very similar; but the teeth of *H. caffer* are considerably longer, stronger, and rather wider proportionately, especially the tubercular teeth.

Length of skull 4 inches; width at zygomatic arch $2\frac{1}{3}$ inches, of middle of brain-case $1\frac{5}{8}$ inch.

Lower jaw very shelving in front, with a prominence on the lower edge under the end of the tooth-line; false grinders 4/4; tubercular moderate, oblong, with two anterior lateral and one larger posterior prominence.

The great difference between the skulls of these two species, which are so like externally, should act as a caution to naturalists, who complain so frequently that species are often separated on too slight external characters. Temminck, for example, would unite *H. ichneumon*, *H. caffer*, and *H. widdringtonii* as one species, and at most only as "*permanent* local varieties," whatever those may be.

3. HERPESTES DORSALIS.

Ichneumon pharaonis, var., A. Smith, S. A. Q. J. 49.

"Back with a narrow, moderately distinct, golden-yellow stripe from nose to tip of tail, and another on each side of the face, which diverges from the front, passes over the eyes, and terminates on the side of the head.

"*Hab.* South Africa.

"Length: head and body 18 inches; tail 15 inches (not adult)."

4. HERPESTES WIDDRINGTONII. B.M.

Like *H. pharaonis*; but fur shorter, under fur more abundant and longer, giving the animal a reddish tint; tail pencilled, distinct, but shorter.

Herpestes widdringtonii, Gray, Ann. Nat. Hist. ix. 49, 1842; Cat. Mamm. B. M. 51; Gerrard, Cat. Ost. B. M. 73; Schinz, Syn. Mamm. i. 375.

Hab. South of Europe: Sierra Morena (*Widdrington*).

5. HERPESTES NUMIDIANUS. B.M.

Herpestes numidianus, F. Cuvier, Mamm. Lith. t.; Verreaux, MS.

Like *H. ichneumon*, but blacker; the rings of the hairs very distinct; throat, legs, and feet black.

Hab. Numidia (*Verreaux*).

6. HERPESTES MADAGASCARIENSIS.

Ichneumon madagascariensis, A. Smith, S. African Quart. Journ. 56.

"Hair of the head, throat, breast, belly, and lower part of the extremities short, that of the other parts longer. The colour of the upper and lateral parts of head and of lower parts of extremities brown red freely speckled with black and white; the upper and lateral parts of the neck, body, and the whole of the tail speckled, being black, brown red and pale reddish white, each hair annulated with these three colours, which are darkest upon the back; throat and lower part of the neck pale tawny; breast, belly, and inner side of extremities dirty pale rufous, speckled with white; woolly hair yellowish white; tail rather thick towards the root, very slender at the point; outer surface of ears thickly covered with short brownish-yellow hairs, inner surface more thickly with a dull tawny sort; whiskers black; nails dark horn-colour. Length of body and head $15\frac{1}{2}$ inches, of tail 14 inches.

" *Hab.* Madagascar (*A. Smith*).

" Size and form of *H. caffer*, but colours much lighter; and when placed side by side, various other differences are evident."

7. ? HERPESTES BENNETTII.

Red brown, slightly grizzled with whitish; tail rather depressed, underside pale red, tip black-pencilled.

Herpestes bennettii, Gray, Loudon's Mag. N. H. i. 578.

Hab. Madagascar (*Mus. Zool. Soc.*). Specimen not to be found.

8. HERPESTES JERDONII. B.M.

Grey, closely and broadly white-ringed; the head darker; the feet darker brown, only slightly annulated; tail conical, with a black pencil of elongated, flaccid, black hairs.

Hab. Asia: Madras (*Jerdon*, 1846).

This is very like *H. ichneumon*, but rather paler.

Length of head and body 19 inches, of tail 17.

Skull (aged) elongated; orbit complete. The false grinders 3/4; the front very small; the second and third triangular, with an internal lobe. The flesh-tooth narrow, elongate; outer edge much longer than the width of the front margin; internal lobe small, slender, on the front edge. Tubercular transverse; first triangular, very short and broad, outer edge oblique, inner part very narrow, acute; second very small, oblong. The hinder part of the palate contracted, with a small wing on each side on the upper, and with an acute keel on each side of the lower edge, ending in a long process behind, with a nodus on the outer side near the end; internal opening narrow, transverse. Lower jaw rather strong; chin shelving, lower edge straight, angle produced, lobe keeled on the inner upper margin. Length of skull about 2″ 3‴ (imperfect), of nose 11‴; width of back of mouth 1″ 1‴.

Ichneumon edwardsii, Geoff. Egypt, 138, from Edw. Birds, 199. t. 199.

Ichneumon major, Geoff. *l. c.* 139, from *Grande mangouste*, Buff. Supp. iii. 173, t. 28. These species are only known from the figures cited.

** *Smaller animal: hair shorter; tail with a small black or red tip.*

9. HERPESTES APICULATUS. B.M.

Fur harsh, dark grey, grizzled with broad black-and-white rings; hair rather elongate, with black tip and a broad white subterminal band; tail with a very slight black tip, from the dark end of the terminal hairs.

Herpestes apiculatus, Gray, Cat. Mamm. B. M. 51.

H. pulverulentus, Wagner, Supp. Schreb. Säugeth. t. 116. f. 2; Schinz, Syn. Mamm. i. 374.

H. caffer, Verreaux, MS.

Length 14 inches; tail 11 inches. (B.M.)

Hab. South Africa, Cape of Good Hope, on rocks near the sea (*A. Smith*).

*** *Smaller animal: hair of body shorter; tail coloured like the back.*

† *African.*

10. HERPESTES PUNCTATISSIMUS.

Fur short; the hairs at the base of the tail twice as long as those of the body; the upper part of the body and limbs pale yellow, dotted with very fine blackish-brown rings, covering all the parts except the chin; the middle part of the neck and belly dirty white; the hairs of the tail, to the extreme point, have many rings; the tip of the tail pale reddish.

Length of head and body 10½ inches, tail 9 inches.

Herpestes punctatissimus, Temm. Esq. Zool. 108.

Hab. Central and Eastern Africa (*Temm.*, *Mus. Leyden.*).

Teeth very strong, much larger than others of the same size.

11. HERPESTES LOEMPO. B.M.

Under fur pale ochraceous; longer hairs black-tipped; fur of head, neck, and back yellow-dotted; back and nape blacker; tail variegated at the base and tufted with long black hairs, which are yellowish at the base; legs deep black.

Herpestes loempo, Temm. Esq. Zool. 93, 1853.
H. mutgigella, Verreaux, MS. (not Rüppell).
Arompo, Bosman, Guinea, 33. f. 8.

In the specimen not in complete fur the ochraceous undercoat is seen through the longer hairs.

Hab. Guinea, near the graves. (Called "Loempo" by a negro at Guinea.)

This species has the toes and other parts of the body, and especially the form of the tail, of *Ichneumon*, but the normal teeth of *Herpestes* (Temm. 94).

The skull is long, ventricose; face and forehead flat, shelving gradually to the back of the orbit, and then shelving in a straight line towards the hinder part of the head. The cavities for the temporal muscles are very large, and they extend in front, and meet together on the crown at a line rather in front of the hinder edge of the orbit. The orbits are large, the hinder edge entire; the hinder part of the skull is broad; the hinder part of the palate between the temporal muscles is narrow and elongate, the hinder opening being nearer the hinder than the front edge of the temporal fossæ. The hinder grinders are slender; the crown of the flesh-tooth is triangular, the front side being the shortest, with the inner tubercle on the straight front edge.

12. Herpestes pluto. B.M.

Black; sides of the head, neck, and front of the body pale brownish, with broad white subterminal bands on the ends of the hairs; hairs harsh; tail black, grey at the base, hairs not ringed at the end; front of thighs, legs, and feet black.

Herpestes pluto, Temm. Esq. Zool. 93, 1853.

Hab. Guinea (*Temminck*); West Coast of Africa (*Gerrard*), adult; ? East Africa (*Verreaux*).

The adult specimens from Gerrard and Verreaux are rather paler than the younger one from Leyden; length of head and body 20 inches, tail 14 inches. Younger from Guinea, length of body and head 16 inches, tail 11 inches. They have also a slight indication of a crest of longer black hairs on the back of the neck.

Skull short, broad; nose shelving; forehead convex; crown flat; orbits complete. False grinders 3/3; first conical, blunt; the second compressed; the third trigonal, with a distinct internal and hinder tubercle. Flesh-tooth rather longer than wide on the front edge; the inner tubercle on front edge, broad, rounded. Tubercular grinders transverse; the front about twice as wide as long, rounded on the inner edge; the second smaller, rather oblong, with two well-marked tubercles, rather narrower and more acute on the hinder part of the inner edge.

Skull—length $3\frac{1}{2}$ inches; width at zygoma $2\frac{1}{10}$ inches, of brain-cavity $1\frac{1}{4}$ inch.

"Like the *H. loempo*; the head and muzzle longer; tail shorter, covered with hairs like those of the body; fur of body, limbs, and tail intense shining black; under fur sombre or dark brown; the fur of the chin, throat, and cheeks black, with very small yellow dots; all the rest intense black. The younger are marked with very fine dots, produced by the yellow rings on the black hairs."—*Temm.*

This does not agree with the specimen (which appears to be changing its teeth) which we received from the Leyden Museum.

13. Herpestes iodoprymnus.

"*Supra ex albido griseoque variegatus, capite, collo, maniculis atque podariis cinerascentibus, hypochondriis viridi-griseis, prymna saturate castanea, pectore, abdomine cristaque unicoloribus ex rufescente isabellinis; cauda longe disticha, basim versus villosissima, supra et infra ad apicem nigrum usque castanea, rhinario et plantis denudatis nigris.*

"Long. tota 24 inches.

Herpestes jodoprymnus, Heuglin, Nov. Acta Leop. xxix. 23.

"*Hab.* Eastern Abyssinia."

14. Herpestes lefebvrii.

Herpestes lefebvrii, DesMurs et Prevost; Heuglin, Nov. Act. Leop. xxix. 23; Lefebvre, Voy. Mamm. t. 1 (not described).

Hab. N.E. Africa (*Heuglin*).

†† *Asiatic.*

15. Herpestes griseus. B.M.

Pale grey, largely white-ringed; head and legs darker; hairs harsh, elongate, with a very broad, white, subterminal ring; feet blackish; tail bushy; cheeks and throat more or less reddish.

Herpestes griseus, Desm. Mamm. 212; Ogilby, Proc. Zool. Soc. 1835; Gray, Cat. Mamm. B. M. 52; Gerrard, Cat. Ost. B. M. 75; Horsfield, Cat. India House Mus. 90.

Ichneumon griseus, Geoff. Egypt. ii. 157.

Mangusta grisea, Fischer, Syn. Mamm. 164.

Herpestes pallidus, Schinz, Syn. Mamm. i. 373.

Viverra grisea, Thunb. Mém. Acad. Pétersb. iii. 306.

Hab. India: Bengal (*Oldham*); Travancore (*P. Poole*); "Sumatra" (*Raffles, Waterh. Cat.*); Dukhun (*Sykes*); Nepal (*Hodgson*).

Var. Paler, with a reddish tinge, and the pale rings rather narrower.

Hab. India (*Hardwick*).

Skull and teeth normal; orbit complete; nose short, thick; false grinders 3—3, first conical, roundish, third triangular. Flesh-tooth rather longer than broad in front. Tubercular transverse; the first with the outer side sloping; the hinder small, oblong, short. Lower jaw shelving in front. Skull—length $2\frac{3}{4}$ inches; width of brain-case $2\frac{3}{24}$ inches, at zygomatic arch $1\frac{5}{12}$ inch.

16. Herpestes persicus. B.M.

Pale ashy, very closely and abundantly black-and-white punctulated; hair short and soft, with black ends and a broad white band near the tip; the chin and underside uniform ashy; tail conical, tapering, coloured like the back; feet like the back, but with shorter hair.

Hab. Persia: Rhugistan and Mohammerah, date-groves (*Kennet, Loftus,* 1853).

Skulls (adult) rather elongate; nose short; forehead very broad, convex; the orbits complete; lower jaw moderately strong, chin shelving. Teeth 40, normal; the third false grinder subtriangular, with small, central, prominent lobe; the flesh-tooth elongate, subtrigonal, the outer side considerably longer than the front one, the inner tubercle small, on the front edge; the front tubercular triangular, transverse, with a very sloping outer edge. Length of skull 2″ 6‴, of nose $7\frac{1}{2}$‴; width of under palate behind $9\frac{1}{2}$‴, of brain-case 10‴, of zygomatic arch 1″ 3‴.

Somewhat like *Calogale nyula*, but much paler and more uniform in dotting; the head shorter and broader, and the tail conical, tapering, thicker at the base.

17. Herpestes fuscus. B.M.

Black brown, white-dotted; hair very long and harsh; ends black, with a narrow pale band very near the tip; throat and belly reddish brown; tail bushy, like the back.

Herpestes fuscus, Waterhouse, P. Z. S. 1838, p. 55; Gerrard, Cat. Ost. B. M. 74; Schinz, Syn. Mamm. i. 372.

Hab. India (*Waterhouse*); Madras (*Jerdon,* 1846).

Mr. Waterhouse's type is in the B. M.: length of body and head 10 inches, tail 17 inches. The one from Madras is smaller.

The skull is intermediate in form between that of *H. ichneumon* and that of *H. paludosus*; the brain-case is nearly of the same external form as the latter, but not quite so ventricose; the orbit is small and rather incomplete behind; the zygomatic arch is rather convex, but, as in *H. ichneumon*, the convexity is more on the hinder end, while it is regularly bowed out in *H. paludosus*. The teeth of the upper jaw are very like those of *H. ichneumon*; but the outer edge of the front tubercular is not so oblique, and the hinder tubercular is even smaller; they are very much slenderer and less bulky than the teeth of *H. paludosus*. Lower jaw very shelving in front; lower edge arched, narrow behind; false grinders 4—4; tubercular oblong, elongate, rather small, crown four-lobed, one lobe at each end and two in the middle portion.

The length of the skull $3\frac{1}{2}$ inches; the width of the brain-case $1\frac{1}{4}$ inch, of the zygomatic arches $1\frac{11}{12}$ inch.

18. Herpestes javanicus. B.M.

Dark black brown, very minutely punctured with yellow; head redder; tail conical; claws short, conical.

Herpestes javanicus, Desm. Mamm. 212; Gray, Cat. Mamm. B. M. 51; Gerrard, Cat. Ost. B. M. 73; Schinz, Syn. Mamm. i. 372; Horsf. Cat. India House Mus. 88.

Mangusta javanica, Horsf. Zool. Java, t.

Mustela galera, Desm. (fide icon. ined.).

Viverra mangusta, Temm.

Ichneumon javanicus, Geoff. Mém. Egypt, ii. 157.

Hab. Java and Sumatra (*Horsfield, Müller*); Penang and Malay peninsula (*Cantor*).

Young.—Pale bay; some of the hair of the tail with long grey tips.

Hab. Sumatra (*Raffles*).

19. Herpestes semitorquatus. B.M.

Dark red brown, very slightly punctulated; cheeks and side of the neck uniform pale bay; legs and feet black; tail black, with some white tips to the hairs.

Length of body and head 18 inches, tail 11 inches.

Herpestes semitorquatus, Gray, Zool. Sulphur, t. 3. f. 1-3, 1849; Gerrard, Cat. Ost. B. M. 74.

Hab. Borneo (*Belcher*).

Like *H. brachyurus* in some respects; but the tail is longer, and the sides of the neck bright pale red, separated from the other parts by a defined line.

The skull is not quite adult, much broader compared with its length than even that of *H. paludosus*. The contraction in the front of the brain-cavity is slight, and rather in front of the back edge of the orbit. The orbit is rather large, and slightly incomplete behind; the zygomatic arch is rather short, and not much bowed out. The teeth are normal, and very like those of *H. ichneumon*; they occupy a rather shorter space. Length of the skull $3\frac{1}{6}$ inches; width of the brain-case $1\frac{5}{12}$, of the zygomatic arch $1\frac{11}{12}$ inch. Skull short and broad.

Lower jaw: chin shelving; lower edge arched, without any prominence under the end of the tooth-line; false grinders 4—4; the front false grinder small, deciduous; the tubercular grinders oblong, longitudinal, with two unequal anterior and one large posterior tubercle.

20. Herpestes exilis.

"*Pallide flavo nigroque annulatis; capite et dorso cinnamomeo et nigro annulatis; pedibus nigrescentibus, gula cinnamomea, ventre pallidiore; cauda pilosa, non penicillata, palmis plantisque nudis.*

"Long. corp. $10\frac{1}{2}$ inches, caudæ 8 inches."

Herpestes exilis, Eydoux, Zool. de la Bonite, t. 3. f. 7-9; Schinz, Syn. Mamm. i. 375.

"*Hab.* East Indies, Touranne (*Eydoux*)."

21. Herpestes malaccensis.

Dull ashy, beneath rather paler; hairs black, white-and-yellow ringed; orbits, ears, and tip of nose naked, violet; tail the colour of the body, very thick at the base, ending with yellow hairs.

Herpestes malaccensis, F. Cuv. Mamm. Lithog. t.
Mangusta malaccensis, Fischer, Syn. 164.
Herpestes pallidus, var., Schinz, Syn. Mamm. i. 373.
H. frederici, Desm. Dict. S. Nat. xxix. 60.
H. leschenaultii, Schinz, Cuv. Thierr. t.
Hab. Malacca, Poudicherry (*Leschenault*).

**** *Smaller; tail like back, much shorter than the body.*

22. Herpestes brachyurus. B.M.

Black, hairs yellow-ringed; under fur brown; face, cheeks, and sides of neck yellower; belly and tail darker; throat pale yellow brown; fore legs and feet blackish; tail thick, about half as long as the body. Length of head and body 18 inches, tail $7\frac{1}{2}$ inches.

Herpestes brachyurus, Gray, Mag. N. H. i. 578, 1836; Voy. of the Samarang, Mam. t. 4. f. 123, 1849; Gerrard, Cat. Ost. B. M. 74.

Mangusta brachyura, De Blainv. Ost. Atlas, t. 6.
Hab. Borneo (Malacca).

The skull is most like that of *H. caffer*, but shorter; the brain-case, the zygomatic arches, and the face are shorter and more ventricose; the forehead broader and regularly convex. The constriction of the front of the brain-case is rather behind the orbit, and not much contracted; the orbit is rather small and complete behind. The teeth are normal, and very like in proportion and form to those of *H. ichneumon*, but rather larger in all parts, as the skull is larger; brain-case five-eighths of entire length.

Length of the skull $3\frac{5}{6}$ inches; width of brain-case $1\frac{2}{6}$ inch, at zygomatic arch $2\frac{1}{12}$ inches.

20. Athylax.

Atilax, F. Cuvier, Mamm. Lithogr. 1826, iii. t.
Athylax, I. Geoff. Mag. Zool. 1837; De Blainv. Plates.
Galera, Brown, Hist. Jam. i. 85, 1756.

Like *Herpestes*, but teeth and jaws stronger. Toes 5—5; claws blunt. Skull elongate. Teeth 40, normal, very massive, with large acute tubercles on the crown; the false grinders 3/4. The lower jaw very strong, with a well-marked chin, and a tubercle on the lower edge under the posterior end of the tooth-line (De Blainv. Ost. Viverra, t. 5). The grinders much longer and broader, with larger and higher tubercles, and the hinder upper tubercular grinder much larger than in most, if not in any other, of the genera; but in the disposition and number of the tubercles they are just like those in the other species.

M. I. Geoffroy compares this genus with his *Galidia*, and concludes that they are distinct (see Mag. de Zool. 1839, p. 25).

This genus is separated from *Herpestes* by the large size and thickness of the teeth and the strength of the lower jaw, with its two distinct prominences. The skull and lower jaw of both species, if they are distinct, are figured by De Blainville, as above referred to.

1. ATHYLAX VANSIRE.

Atilax vansire, F. Cuvier, Mamm. Lithog. 411. t.; Dict. Sci. Nat. t.

Mustela galera, Erxl. Syst. 453; Schreb. Säugeth. t. 155.

Viverra galera, Shaw.

Herpestes galera, Desm. Mamm. 212; Wagner, Gel. Anzeig. ix.

Mangusta galera, Fischer, Syn. 165.

Mangouste vansire, Geoff.

Mangusta (*Athylax*) *galera*, De Blainv. Ostéogr. Viverra, t. 5 (skull).

Ichneumon vansire, A. Smith, S. A. Q. J. 53.

I. galera, Geoff. Hist. Egypt, 138.

Vansire, Buffon, H. N. xiii. 157, t. 21.

Hab. Madagascar.

According to De Blainville's figure, the skull is more solid and stronger than that of *A. paludosus*.

Temminck thinks this a variety or local state of *Herpestes paludosus* (Esq. Zool. 100).

The description of the *Vansire*, from a stuffed specimen, is as follows:—"The fur is less long than that of a Marten or Polecat, of the same dark brown colour on all parts of the body; the under fur is brown; the longer hairs are brown at the roots; the remainder blackish and reddish, which succeed each other at small intervals to the tip. These two colours occupy all the length of the hairs of the tail. Toes 5—5. Length of body and head 13 inches, tail 7 inches, hair $2\frac{1}{2}$ inches long. Madagascar."—*Buffon, H. N.* xiii. 169, t. 21.

In the figure, the claws are represented as long, compressed, arched, acute.

The skull of the animal figured by F. Cuvier is engraved in De Blainv. Ostéogr. t. 5.

2. ATHYLAX PALUDOSUS. B.M.

Brown, closely yellow-punctulated; hair elongate.

Herpestes paludosus, Cuv. R. A.; Gray, Cat. Mamm. B. M. 52; Gerrard, Cat. Ost. B. M. 74.

Mangusta urinatrix, A. Smith, Zool. Journ. iv. 237.

H. palustris, Rüppell.

H. griseus, Burchell, Cat.

H. caffer, Mus. Stuttgard.

H. paludinosus, Peters, Reise Mossamb. Säugeth. 119.

H. atilax (partly), Schinz, Syn. Mamm. i. 371.

Ichneumon urinatrix, A. Smith, S. African Quart. Journ. i. 51.

Mangusta paludinosa, De Blainv. Ostéog. Viverra, t. 5 (skull), t. 12 (teeth).

Hab. S. Africa, Cape of Good Hope, on the banks of the rivers; a great diver (*A. Smith*); E. Africa, Quillimane (*Peters*).

Var. Black-brown, only very slightly punctulated, except on the side of the throat.

Var. Canine teeth very strong,

Hab. Guinea (*Gervais*).

The skull is wider, compared with its length, than in most species of the genus; the brain-case is more convex; the contraction in the front of the brain-case is not so great or so sudden as in *Herpestes ichneumon* and *H. caffer*, and is only a very small distance behind the hinder edge of the orbit. The orbit is very incomplete behind. The teeth are normal; they are all much more bulky and broader than in any of the other species of the genus which I have seen; the hinder upper false grinder is triangular, with nearly equal sides; the flesh-tooth is very strong, the front edge being nearly four-fifths of the length on the outer side; the first tubercular is not twice as broad as the length of the outer edge. The brain-case is about five-eighths of the entire length. The hinder part of the palate contracted, flat, with a diverging crest on each side above, and a ridge on each side below, with the aperture transverse, in a line with the base of the lateral crest. The bullæ large, vesicular, rounded below and behind.

Length of the skull $3\frac{1}{12}$ inches; width of brain-case $1\frac{1}{12}$ inch, at zygomatic arch $2\frac{1}{6}$ inches.

The zygomatic arch, in comparative length and convexity, is very like that of the skull of *H. ichneumon.*

Lower jaw strong, short, with a distinct chin-angle in front; teeth very large and strong; tubercular oblong, longitudinal, large, with two anterior and one broad hinder lobe, the angle behind with flattened expanded processes.

3. ATHYLAX ROBUSTUS. B.M.

Brown, very minutely and closely punctured; the head blacker, with a subvertical band; the edge of the lower jaw and cheeks under the ears yellowish, not punctulated; legs and feet nearly black; tail black brown, punctulated.

Hab. Africa: "White Nile" (no. 6168, adult; no. 6169, younger) (*Parzudaki*).

Very like *A. paludosus*, but paler, and with the pale cheeks; the teeth are very large and strong, like those of the *A. paludosus* variety from Guinea.

Lower jaw like that of *A. paludosus*, but not quite so strong, and more sloping in front; the compressed teeth rather large; the tubercular oblong, elongate, moderate, with two large lobes in front, and one larger behind.

Skull elongate; nose short, thick; forehead convex; orbits complete. Teeth 36; the false grinders 2/3, with a short space between the canine and the first false molar, where a small tooth may have fallen out. The false grinders triangular, with a triangular tubercle on the middle of the inner side. The flesh-tooth massive, triangular, nearly as wide in front as long on the outer side, with a large internal tubercle on a line with the front edge. Tubercular

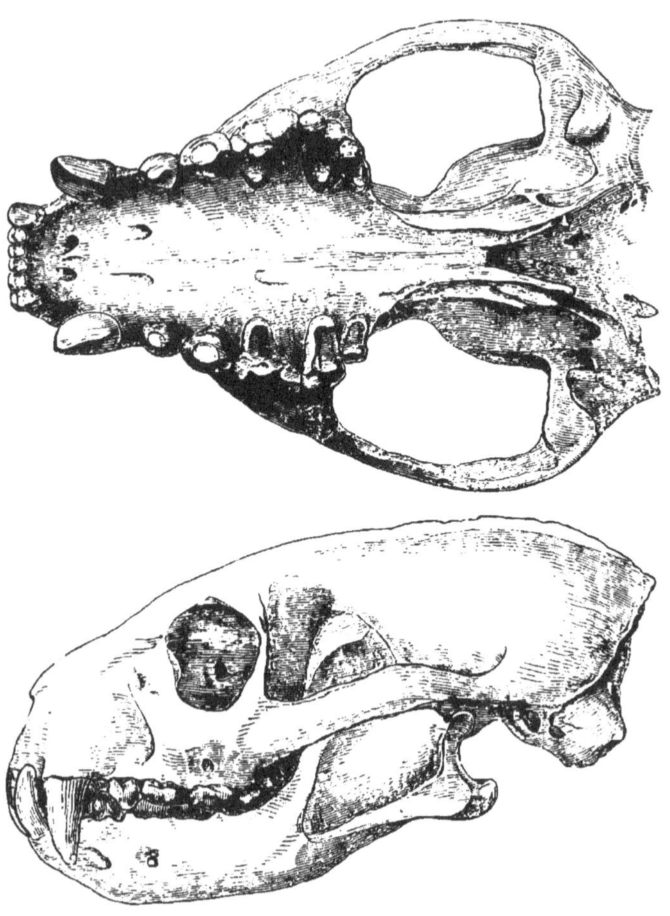

Skull of *Athylax robustus.*

grinders transverse; the front triangular, much wider than long, outer edge oblique, inner edge narrow; hinder one oblong, much smaller. The hinder part of the palate produced nearly to a line with the condyles, keeled on each side, and with a strong keel on each side of the lower surface, edging the very narrow contracted hinder opening. Ear-bullæ very large, vesicular, rounded below and behind. Lower jaw strong, solid, nearly as high behind as in front; chin shelving; gonyx long, the angle produced, bent up at the end, and keeled on the outer lower edge. Length of skull $4\frac{6}{12}$ inches, of nose 1½ inch; width of brain-case 1½ inch, of back of mouth 1½ inch, of zygomatic arch 2½ inches.

21. CALOGALE.

Body elongate. Tail very long, slender, cylindrical, covered with short hair, with longer at the tip. Toes 5—5; claws short, triangular, acute. Pupil linear, erect. Skull elongate; brain-case elongate, two-thirds the length of skull (see Peters, Reise, t. 28). Teeth 40; false grinders 2/3, 2/3, compressed; flesh-tooth narrow, much longer than broad, with inner tubercles on front edge; tubercular grinders $\frac{2-2}{1-1}$, transverse, hinder very small.

* *Tail like back, rather thick.*

1. CALOGALE NYULA. B.M.

Pale grey, very closely and minutely black-and-white punctulated; tail elongate, rather tapering, coloured like the back.

Herpestes nyula, Hodgson, J. A. S. Beng. 1836, p. 236; Gray, Cat. Mamm. B. M. 52; Gerrard, Cat. Ost. B. M. 75; Horsf. Cat. India House Mus. 92.
H. pallidus (partly), Schinz, Syn. Mamm. i. 373.
H. nigula, Hodgson, Calcutta Journ. N. H. iv. 287.
Hab. India: Nepal, Open Tarai (*Hodgson*); Salt Range (*Oldham*).
Length of head and body 15 inches, tail 12 inches.
The largest species of the genus, but much smaller than *Herpestes griseus*, which it somewhat resembles.
Skull very like *H. griseus*, but nose longer; orbit complete, and more compressed and tapering; the flesh-tooth and the front tubercular grinder rather larger and more massive.
Skull—length 2¾ inches; width at brain-case 1 inch, at zygomatic arch 1⅓ inch.
These animals have the tail rather more bushy than the more typical *Calogale*; but they have the narrow skull and longer narrow brain-case and slender narrow flesh-tooth of the genus.

2. CALOGALE NEPALENSIS. B.M.

Dark grey, very minutely and closely punctulated, with black and pale-whitish hairs, with a broad subterminal pale band; tail subcylindrical, pencilled at the end, coloured like the back.
Length 13 inches, tail 11 inches.

Herpestes nepalensis, Gray, Mag. N. H. 578, 1836; Hodgson, J. A. S. Beng. 235; Gerrard, Cat. Osteol. B. M. 74; Horsfield, Cat. India House Mus. 91.
H. auropunctatus, Hodgson, J. A. Soc. Beng. i. 578; Schinz, Syn. Mamm. i. 373.
H. javanicus, Hodgson.
H. griseus, Hodgson, Journ. Asiat. Soc. Beng. xiv. 346.
H. pallipes, Blyth, J. Asiat. Soc. Beng. xiv. 346.

Hab. India: Nepal, hill regions (*Hodgson*); Assam (*M'Clelland*); Affghanistan (*Griffith*).

Skull—orbit complete, like *C. grisea* and *C. nyula*, but smaller; the nose short, like *C. grisea*, but more compressed; teeth normal, very like *C. nyula*, the hinder tubercular being larger than in *C. grisea*.

Skull, length $1\frac{5}{12}$ inch; width at brain-case $\frac{4}{5}$ inch, at zygoma $1\frac{1}{4}$ inch.

3. Calogale rutila. B.M.

Grizzled chestnut-brown, variegated with black and white rings on the hairs; head and limbs darker chestnut, with scarcely any, or very narrow, white rings; lips and throat and under part of the body uniform duller brown, not grizzled; ears brown; the nape with longer hairs, forming broad short crests.

Herpestes rutilus, Gray, P. Z. S. 1861, p. 136.

Hab. Cambogia (*Mouhot*), one specimen.

4. Calogale microcephala.

Head very small; teeth very small; ears close, short; nose very short and narrow. Fur finely dotted all over, deep brown and dull yellow, of the under part dirty white; the under fur ashy at the base, with a very broad yellow band; the hairs silky, blackish brown, with small ochraceous rings; the hairs of the tail with broader rings, those of the tip similar.

Length of head and body 10 inches, of tail $9\frac{1}{2}$ inches.

Herpestes microcephalus, Temm. Esq. Zool. 113.

Hab. ——? (*Mus. Leyden, procured at Havre*).

** *Tail-end bright bay, very slender.*

5. Calogale sanguinea.

Head ashy, black-dotted; body isabella-red; hair with tip and rings brown; throat, chest, and belly white; feet pale; tail isabella and black, varied, tip bright red brown.

Length of head and body $11\frac{1}{2}$ inches, of tail $12\frac{1}{2}$ inches.

Herpestes sanguineus, Rüpp. Fauna Abyss. 27, t. 8 & 10 (skull); Schinz, Syn. Mamm. i. 370.

Hab. Abyssinia.

6. Calogale grantii. B.M.

Pale yellow brown, nearly uniform, very slightly grizzled, with white tips to the hairs; end of tail bay.

Herpestes badius, Sclater, P. Z. S. 1864, p. 100.

Hab. East Africa: Mgunda Mkali (*Capt. Speke*).

*** *Tail-end black, very slender.*

7. Calogale mutgigella. B.M.

Dark olive-brown, very minutely punctulated; tail-end black.

Length of body and head 13½ inches, of tail 11½ inches.

Herpestes mutgigella, Rüpp. Fauna Abyss. t. 9. f. 1; Gray, Cat. Mamm. B. M. 51; Gerrard, Cat. Osteol. B. M. 75; Schinz, Syn. Mamm. i. 370.

Hab. Abyssinia.

Skull rather elongate, narrow, like that of *C. nyula*; nose flat; forehead and crown in one line; brain-case ovate, flat-topped, contracted in the front over the orbit; orbit incomplete; false grinders 2–3/3, front small, hinder rather compressed, with a small internal and a small hinder acute tubercle; flesh-tooth much longer than broad—inner tubercles small, on front edge; tubercular grinders transverse, the first trigonal, the outer edge broader, the inner narrow, acute; the second very small, nearly like the first in form.

Skull 2½ inches wide at the broadest part; brain-case 1 inch.

8. CALOGALE ORNATA.

Herpestes ornatus, Peters, Monatsb. Akad. Berlin, 1852, p. 81; Reise n. Mossamb. Säugeth. i. 117, t. 26, 1852; Gerrard, Cat. Osteol. B. M. 75; Temm. Esq. Zool. 115.

Hab. Eastern Africa: Tete, lat. 17 (*Smith*).

The figure is very like *C. mutgigella*; but the grizzling of the back seems to form more irregularly waved cross streaks; perhaps this is only the attempt of the artist to represent the grizzling. The figure of the skull also resembles that of the former species.

Temminck regards this as a variety of *C. mutgigella* (Esq. Zool. 116).

9. CALOGALE PUNCTULATA. B.M.

Reddish grey, minutely black-and-grey punctured; face redder; under fur black; long hairs brown, upper half whitish, with a broad black subapical band and a bay tip; tail-end black; front claw rather slender, acute; inner toes very short, claws short.

Herpestes punctulatus, Gray, P. Z. S. 1849, p. 11.

H. badius, var. 2, Temm. Esq. Zool. 105.

Hab. South-east Africa: Port Natal (*Williams*).

Like *C. mutgigella*, but redder; face red bay.

10. CALOGALE MELANURA. B.M.

Reddish brown, minute, punctulate; hair short; tail-end black; front claws acute, short.

Cynictis melanura, Martin, P. Z. S. 1830, p. 56; Fraser, Zool. Typica, t.; Gerrard, Cat. Ost. B. M. 77; Schinz, Syn. Mamm. i. 377.

Herpestes melanura, Gray, P. Z. S. 1838, p. 5.

H. badius, var. 3, Temm. Esq. Zool. 107.

Hab. West Africa, Sierra Leone (*Capt. P. L. Strachan*); Damara Land (*Alexander*).

Var.? Rather paler (not in good state). B.M.

Herpestes ochromeles, Pucheran (*fide* Verreaux).

Hab. "Central Africa" (*Verreaux*).

Skull elongate, very much contracted in front over the orbit; the flesh-tooth trigonal, longer than broad; hinder tubercular very minute, transverse.

11. CALOGALE BADIA. B.M.

Bright bay, nearly uniform; end of tail black.

Young? pale brown, with an obscure waved appearance from the broad bands on the hairs.

Herpestes badius, A. Smith, Illust. Zool. S. A. Mamm. t. 4, ♀; Gray, Cat. Mamm. B. M. 51; Gerrard, Cat. Ost. B. M. 74; Schinz, Syn. Mamm. i. 373; Temm. Esq. Zool. 98?

Ichneumon ratlamuchi, A. Smith, App. Report, 1836, p. 42.

Herpestes cawii, A. Smith.

Hab. South Africa, on plains away from the sea; ? Guinea (called "Koukeboe") (*Temm.*), perhaps a variety or species.

M. Temminck thinks that *Herpestes punctatus* and *Cynictis melanura* are varieties of this species (Temm. Esq. Zool. 100).

Skull rather elongate, compressed; brain-case elongate, contracted in front; orbit complete in the adult, incomplete in the young. The false grinders 3—3; the first very small; second compressed, conical; third subcompressed, placed obliquely, with a very minute, scarcely appreciable internal lobe, and no hinder one. Flesh-tooth trigonal, considerably longer than broad; the internal lobe small, on the front edge. The first tubercular grinder transverse, outer edge oblique, inner (narrower) rounded; the second very minute, linear, with two tubercles.

12. CALOGALE VENATICA. B.M.

Dark bay, white-grizzled, the longer hairs white-tipped; tail-end black.

Herpestes badius, var., Gray, P. Z. S. 1849, p. 11; Peters, Reise n. Mossamb. Säugeth. 119.

Hab. East Africa.

13. CALOGALE GRACILIS. B.M.

Brown or blackish brown, scarcely grizzled; fur on side of the neck shorter and very minutely grizzled; end of tail blacker.

Herpestes gracilis, Rüppell, Fauna Abyss. t. 8. f. 1, t. 10; Schinz, Syn. Mamm. i. 369.

Ichneumia gracilis, I. Geoff. Mag. Zool. 1839, p. 17; Gray, Cat. Mamm. B. M. 53; Gerrard, Cat. Ost. B, M. 76.

I. nigricaudatus, I. Geoff. MS., *l. c.* 18.

Hab. Abyssinia (*Rüppell*).

M. I. Geoffroy objects to the name, because this species is stouter than the other *Herpestæ*; he does not appear to have seen any specimen. (Mag. Zool. 1839, p. 18).

14. CALOGALE? THYSANURA.

Minor, pilis fusco et pallide luteo annulatis; pedibus fuscis; cauda longa, penicillo magno aterrimo terminata.

Length of head and body 12 inches, of tail 13 inches.

Herpestes thysanurus, Wagner, München. gelehrt. Anz. ix. 449; Schreb. Säugeth. Supp. ii. p. 301; Schinz, Syn. Mamm. i. 368.

Hab. India: Cashmere.

22. GALERELLA.

Body slender. Legs short. Tail elongate, slender, tapering, covered with shortish hairs. Toes 5—4. Claws short, compressed, acute. Skull elongate; brain-case rather ventricose. Face short. Teeth 38; false grinders 3/3, 3/3; flesh-tooth triangular, longer than broad; tubercular grinders 2/1, 2/1, transverse.

GALERELLA OCHRACEA. B.M.

Pale brown, minutely punctulated; throat, underside, and inside of the limbs white; tail-end black; front thumb very small, low down.

Cynictis ochraceus, Gerrard, Cat. Ost. B. M. 77.

Herpestes ochraceus, Gray, P. Z. S. 1848, p. 138, pl. VIII.; Ann. & Mag. N. H. 1849, iv. 376.

H. mutgigella, var., Temm. Esq. Zool. 116.

Hab. East Africa: Abyssinia (*F. H. Hora*).

M. Temminck regards this as only a seasonal state of *H. mutgigella* (Esq. Zool. 116), not observing that it has no internal toe on the hind feet.

Skull elongate; brain-case rather ventricose; face short, forehead arched; flesh-tooth triangular, much longer than broad, inner tubercle anterior; false grinders $\frac{3-3}{2-2}$; the hinder tubercular very small; orbit incomplete behind; not so contracted in front over the back of the orbit. Like *Calogale badia* in size, but brain-case more ventricose.

23. CALICTIS.

The pupil oblong, transverse. Claws rather arched, compressed. Tail thick, conical, tapering. Ears rounded. Skull elongate. Face short. Teeth 40; false grinders $\frac{3-3}{4-4}$; the flesh-tooth triangular, scarcely longer than broad; tubercular grinders $\frac{2-2}{1-1}$.

The skull elongate, rather narrow, much contracted in front of the brain-case; orbit rather incomplete; the nose shelving; crown flat. The false grinders 3/3; the first very small; second compressed; third trigonal, with a small internal and a small hinder lobe. The flesh-tooth triangular, scarcely longer than broad in front, the inner lobe on the front edge. Tubercular grinders transverse; the first subtrigonal, oblique, much broader than long; the second very minute.

The skull 3 inches long, and brain-cavity $1\frac{1}{8}$ inch broad behind.

CALICTIS SMITHII. B.M.

Reddish brown, very closely pale-grizzled, hair with red-brown ends, and subconical white bands; feet and tip of tail black.

Herpestes smithii, Gray, Loudon's Mag. N. Hist. 1837, i. 2; Cat. Mamm. B. M. 51; Proc. Zool. Soc. 1851, p. 131, pl. XXXI.; Ann. & Mag. N. H. 1853, xii. 47; Gerrard, Cat. Ost. B. M. 74; Temm. Esq. Zool. 97.

Hab. Ceylon (*A. Grace*).

M. Temminck, misled by some dealer, believes that this animal inhabits Cape Coast and Guinea. He complains of the shortness of my diagnosis; but says himself it is well characterized by a shorter but nearly identical one (see Temm. Esq. Zool. 98).

24. ARIELA.

Helogale (part.), Gray, P. Z. S. 1861, p. 308.

Body elongate. Tail slender, elongated, subcylindrical, thickest at the base. Toes 5—5. Skull elongate. Face short. Teeth 40; false grinders $\frac{2-2}{3-3}$; flesh-tooth trigonal, rather broader than long, inner lobe long, rounded, on front edge; tubercular grinders 2/1, 2/1.

ARIELA TÆNIONOTA. B.M. (skull only).

Hair of head, under part of neck, and lower part of the extremities short, elsewhere pretty long; centre of the face, forehead, crown, cheeks, and space between the eyes and ears black, freely pencilled with white. Muzzle, upper and lower lips, and space under lower jaw light chestnut; outer surface of the ears brownish, inner surface dirty reddish white; back and sides of neck, shoulders, anterior part of back and sides, and outer surface of anterior extremities finely pencilled black and white; the rest of back and upper part of sides banded transversely deep black and yellowish white or light yellow-brown; flanks and outer surface of hinder extremities towards the body pencilled dull black and yellowish white; lower part of neck, breast, belly, and lower surface of extremities black; tail slender, thickest towards the root, for about two-thirds of its length pencilled black-brown and pale ferruginous; last third nearly uniform black.

Length of head and body 15 inches, of tail 7½ inches.

Helogale tænionota, Gray, P. Z. S. 1861, p. 308; Gerrard, Cat. Ost. B. M. 76.

Herpestes tænionotus, A. Smith, S. African Journ. 52, 1834.

H. zebra (partly), Schinz, Syn. Mamm. i. 371.

Ichneumon tænionotus, A. Smith, S. Afr. Quart. Journ. 50.

Hab. South Africa: Natal (*A. Smith*).

The flesh-tooth broader than long; the inner lobe long, rounded, on the front edge. The first false grinders conical, compressed; the second trigonal, with an internal tubercle. The tubercular grinders transverse; the first large, with a long internal lobe, rather thinner, narrower than the outer edge, and rounded within. Orbit incomplete behind. Skull elongate.

25. Ichneumia.

Ichneumia, I. Geoff. Compt. Rend. 1837, p. 582; Mag. Zool. 1839, pp. 13 & 31.

Lasiopus, I. Geoff. Cour. d'Hist. Nat. des Mamm. 57, 1835.

Body compressed. Legs rather long. Fur grizzled. Tail conical, bushy. Toes 5—5. Claws rather elongate, sharp. The greater part of the soles of the hind feet are covered with hair. Teeth 40; false grinders $\frac{3-3}{4-4}$; flesh-tooth triangular; tubercular grinders $\frac{2-2}{1-1}$.

The most Viverrine form of this subtribe.

M. Geoffroy separates this genus on account of its peculiar dentition, which he describes:—false grinders 3/4, true 1/1, tubercular 2/1 (Mag. Zool. 1839, p. 7). M. Geoffroy's figures are lower on their legs and more vermiform than our specimen of *I. albicauda.*

Dr. A. Smith, when first describing this species, observed, "Its teeth exhibit a slight difference in form, and are not so closely set as in the true Ichneumons. This peculiarity, in addition to the state of the soles of the feet, may, when its manners and habits are better known, require it to be separated from the present genus" (South African Quart. Journ. 52, 1834).

"Shorter and more robust, and stands higher on its limbs, than *Herpestes.*"—*A. Smith.*

1. Ichneumia albicauda. B.M.

Tail white, nearly to the base.

Ichneumia albicauda, I. Geoff. Mag. Zool. 1839, p. 13, 35, t. 11; Gray, Cat. Mamm. B. M. 53.

Herpestes albicaudus, Cuvier, Règ. Anim. ed. 2, 1834.

H. albicaudatus, A. Smith, S. Afr. Quart. Journ, 181, 1834; Schinz, Syn. Mamm. i. 369.

Mangusta albicauda, De Blainv. Ostéogr. Viverra, t. 12 (teeth).

Hab. Africa: Port Natal (*A. Smith*); Senegal (*Heudelot*); Galam (*Delambre*).

2. Ichneumia leucura.

Herpestes leucurus, Ehrenb. Sym. Phys. Mamm. t. 12, cop. Schreb. Säugeth. t. 116; Rüppell, Abyss. Fauna, i. 27; Peters, Reise n. Mossamb. Säugeth. 119; Schinz, Syn. Mamm. i. 369.

Hab. East Africa: Nubia and Dongola (*Ehrenb.*).

This may be the same as the preceding. See observations of M. I. Geoffroy, Mag. Zool. 1839, p. 14, note.

3. Ichneumia albescens.

Pale brown; tip of tail white.

Ichneumia albescens, I. Geoff. Mag. Zool. 1839, p. 35, t. 12; Gerrard, Cat. Ost. B. M. 76.

Hab. East Africa: Sennaar (*Botta*).

Skull ovate, swollen; the brain-cavity one-half the length; nose shelving; forehead and crown rather convex; orbit incomplete behind. False grinders 3/3 ; the third triangular, sides of equal length, with an internal tubercle on the hinder edge. The flesh-tooth triangular, rather longer than wide in front, narrow behind ; the internal tubercle anterior, rounded internally. The tubercular grinders large, oblong, trigonal, about half as wide again as long; the hinder rather the smallest (see I. Geoff. Mag. Zool. 1839, t. 13).

In the figure the brain-cavity is half the length of the skull, and the skull is as wide at the widest part of the zygomatic arch as the length of the brain-cavity.

4. ICHNEUMIA NIGRICAUDA.

Ichneumia nigricauda, Pucheran, Rev. et Mag. Zool. vii. 39; Arch. für Naturg. 1856, p. 43.

Hab. Senegal.

26. BDEOGALE.

Bdeogale, W. Peters, Reise n. Mossamb. Mamm. 119 (1850).

Toes 4—4, short. Heel hairy to the soles. Claws compressed. Tail bushy. Skull, orbits incomplete behind (t. 27 & 28). False grinders 3—3 ; hinder broad, triangular. Flesh-tooth triangular, broad ; sides nearly equal ; angles rounded (t. 27. f. 4).

Hab. Africa.

The teeth are like those of *Rhinogale*, and the nose is rather produced and rounded below in the figure; so that perhaps this genus ought to be arranged near to it; but it differs from it in having four toes on each foot.

1. BDEOGALE CRASSICAUDA.

Blackish-ashy hair, black-and-white ringed; limbs and tail black.

Bdeogale crassicauda, W. Peters, Monatsb. K. Akad. Berl. 1852, p. 81; Reise n. Mossamb. Mamm. 120, t. 27; Temm. Esq. Zool. 115; Gerrard, Cat. Ost. B. M. 72.

Hab. East Africa: Tete, Boror (*Peters, Mus. Berlin*).

2. BDEOGALE PUISA.

Brown hairs, black-and-yellow ringed; limbs and tail blackish brown.

Bdeogale puisa, W. Peters, Monatsb. K. Akad. Berl. 1852, p. 82; Reise n. Mossamb. Mamm. 124, t. 28; Temm. Esq. Zool. 115; Gerrard, Cat. Ost. B. M. 72.

Hab. East Africa: Mossimboa (*Peters, Mus. Berlin*).

3. BDEOGALE NIGRIPES.

"Body whitish; tail snow-white; feet black."

Bdeogale nigripes, Pucheran, Rev. et Mag. Zool. vii. 111; Arch. für Naturg. 1856, p. 44.

Hab. Gaboon (*Aubry Lecomte, Mus. Paris*).

"Larger than the other species."

27. Urva.

Urva, Hodgson; Gray, Cat. Mam. B. M. 50.
Mesobema, Hodgson.

Head broad. Ears rounded. Nose rather produced, with a longitudinal groove beneath. Body elongate. Legs short. Tail conical, attenuated, covered with long hairs. Toes 5—5; claws compressed, rather short, curved; inner toes of fore and hind feet very short, with short claws rather high up the foot. Claws brown. Hind part of the soles of hind feet covered with hair, that is bent towards the centre on each side. The front part bald, oblong, narrow behind, occupying less than two-thirds of the foot, with three subequal pads in front and two elongated pads on each side of the hinder edge (Hodgson, J. A. S. B. t. 31. f. 5). Front upper false grinders 2, compressed; the third subtriangular, with a very small subposterior internal tubercle, and a small posterior marginal one; flesh-tooth large, elongate, triangular, nearly twice as long as the front margin, with a large internal lobe on the front edge; tubercular grinders transverse, twice as broad as long on the outer edge; hinder tubercular very small, oblong, transverse.

Urva cancrivora. The Urva. B.M.

Black-grizzled, hairs with a very broad white subterminal ring; a white streak on the side of the neck; legs and feet black; tail ashy red at the end.

Urva cancrivora, Hodgson, Journ. Asiat. Soc. Beng. vi. 560; Gray, Cat. Mamm. B. M. 50; Gerrard, Cat. Ost. B. M. 73; Schinz, Syn. Mamm. i. 358; Horsfield, Cat. India House Mus. 93.

Mesobema cancrivorus, Hodgson, Journ. Asiat. Soc. Bengal, x. 910; Calcutta Journ. N. H. ii. 214, iv. 287.

Gulo urva, Hodgson, Journ. Asiat. Soc. Beng. v. 238; Calcutta Journ. N. H. ii. 45, t. 13½. f. 2.

Hab. India—Nepal, in caverns, Central Northern region (*Hodgson*); Affghanistan (*Griffith*); Arakan (*Blyth*).

Fur lax, elongate, ringed, blackish ashy, more or less grizzled by the white tips to the hairs; lips and cheeks whitish; a long streak on the side of neck white; legs and feet black; tail bushy, appearing more or less irregularly banded from the dark band on the hairs.

The not quite adult skull of *Urva cancrivora* is very like that of *Teniogale vitticollis*, but considerably smaller. The orbit is incomplete. The zygomatic arches not so bowed out, with most convex part nearer the hinder end. The nose is rather thick. The contraction of the brain-case is just over the hinder part of the orbit; the brain-case is rather longer (perhaps $\frac{1}{10}$th) than the face. The teeth are normal, and very like in form and proportion to those of *T. vitticollis*; but they are rather narrower, and the first tubercular molar is shorter and broader, more oblong, and the hinder tubercular molar smaller. Length of the skull 3½ inches; width of the brain-case 1⅙ inch, of the zygomatic arch 2 inches.

Lower jaw slender; chin gradually shelving; the lower edge

curved, arched up behind, to near the condyle behind. The false grinders 4—4; the front small, concave. Tubercular grinders moderate, oblong, elongate, with two small anterior and two large high posterior prominences.

In the 'Illustrations of Indian Zoology' I figured an animal under the name of *Viverra ? fusca*, from one of General Hardwick's drawings. In the 'Ann. & Mag. Nat. Hist.,' 1842, p. 260, I proposed for it a genus named *Osmetectis*. As yet I have never seen or heard of an animal from India that agrees with the figure. It has been supposed that it may be *Urva cancrivora* of Hodgson; but it does not well represent that species.

28. TÆNIOGALE.

Mungos, sp.?, Ogilby, P. Z. S. 1835, p. 103.

Whiskers weak, slender. Nose grooved beneath. Toes 5—5. Claws compressed, rather elongate, very acute. Thumb short; claw distinct, rather elevated. Great toes very short, indistinct, with a small claw; hinder claws broader. Soles of the hind feet quite bald to the heel. Ears rounded. Skull oval. Teeth 42; false grinders 3/4, 3/4, first conical, second and third with three unequal tubercles; tubercular grinders $\frac{2-2}{1-1}$, first upper triangular, large, second short, twice as broad as long (Ogilby, *l. c.*).

Mr. Ogilby described this animal as having 42 teeth, 3 false grinders in the upper, and 4 in the lower jaw. Perhaps one tooth in the lower jaw was in exchange.

TÆNIOGALE VITTICOLLIS. B.M.

Black, red-washed; hair very long, soft, black, with long red tips; head black, minutely punctulated; legs and feet black; tail black; streak on side of throat black; the front claw elongate, compressed, arched.

Mungos vitticollis, Gray, Cat. Mam. B. M. 50 (not Ogilby); Gerrard, Cat. Ost. B. M. 72.

Herpestes vitticollis, Bennett, P. Z. S. 1835, p. 67; Madras Journ. 1839, p. 103, t. 2; Schinz, Syn. Mamm. 374; Temm. Esq. Zool. 111.

Mangusta vitticollis, Elliot, Madras Journ. of Lit. & Sci. 1840, p. 12, t. 1; De Blainv. Ostéogr. 48, t. 96.

Mungos ? vitticollis, Ogilby, P. Z. S. 1835, p. 103.

Hab. India: Madras, in thick forests (*W. Elliot*); Travancore (*P. Poole*).

Varies in the greyness of the fur and the extent and darkness of the red bay on the sides of the neck and body, there being least on the specimens that have the most grey and distinctly white rigid hairs. In some specimens (perhaps in some seasons) the whole animal has a bright bay tint from the tips of the longest hairs.

The skull is elongate, like that of *Athylax paludosus*; but the brain-case is more ventricose and higher, and the orbit smaller and complete behind. The zygomatic arch is rather short and very much bowed out, the most convex part of the arch being rather behind the middle of its length. The contraction of the brain-case is rather behind the back of the orbit. The teeth are normal, nearly as massive as, and agreeing very generally in proportion of parts and position or form of the internal lobes with those of *A. paludosus*; but they are rather slender and longer comparatively in all their parts. The palate also is much narrower and longer. The third upper false molar has a small central internal lobe. The front edge of the flesh-tooth is fully two-thirds the length of the outer edge; the hinder lobe of it is narrow, and angular behind. The front tubercular molar has a very oblique outer edge. The brain-case is rather more than half the entire length.

The length of the skull $3\frac{3}{4}$ inches; the width of the brain-case $1\frac{5}{12}$ inch, of the zygomatic arch $2\frac{1}{4}$ inches.

The lower jaw broad in front, narrow behind, without any tubercles on the lower edge under the end of the tooth-line. False grinders 4—4; the front very small, curved, close at the front of the second. The tubercular grinder very large, oblong, subcircular, with two large unequal tubercles on the front and a very large one on the hinder part of the crown.

The lower jaw of *Urva* is distinguished from that of the genus *Herpestes* by having no prominence or tubercle on the lower edge under the hinder end of the tooth-line.

29. Onychogale.

Body slender. Tail conical, hairy, about as long as the body. Toes 5—5; inner toes small; front claws very long, compressed, curved. Teeth 40; false grinders 3/4, 3/4.

The hinder end of the skull deeply and sharply notched, instead of being transversely truncated as in the small *Herpestes*. The notch in the living animal is filled up with a cartilaginous septum.

Onychogale maccarthiæ. B.M.

Red brown; hair elongate, flaccid, pale brown, with a broad, thick, subterminal band and a long whitish-brown tip; fur of hands and face shorter. Feet blackish brown; hair white-tipped. Tail redder; hair elongate, red, one-coloured. Ears rounded, hairy.

Herpestes maccarthiæ, Gray, B. M.; Gerrard, Cat. Osteol. B. M. 75.

Cynictis maccarthiæ, Gray, P. Z. S. 1851, p. 131, Mamm. pl. xxxi.; Ann. & Mag. N. H. 1853, xii. 47.

Herpestes fulvescens, Kelaart, Ceylon.

Hab. Ceylon (*Lady Maccarthy*).

30. Helogale.

Helogale, Gray, P. Z. S. 1861, p. 308; Arch. für Naturg. xxviii. (1862) p. 128.

Body slender. Head oval. Ears distant. Toes 5—5; the inner

toe small; front claws rather elongate, compressed, acute. Soles of the hind feet partly bald. Tail conical, covered with elongate hairs. Skull short, broad. Face short. Teeth 36 (see P. Z. S. 1861, p. 308, fig.); false grinders $\frac{2-2}{3-3}$; the flesh-tooth triangular; tubercular grinders $\frac{2-2}{1-1}$.

Herpestes tænionotus, A. Smith, which I referred to this genus, is distinct.

1. HELOGALE PARVULA. B.M.

Fur uniform blackish brown, very minutely pale-punctulated. Length of body and head 7 inches, of tail 7 inches.

Helogale parvulus, Gray, P. Z. S. 1861, p. 308 (fig. skull); Gerrard, Cat. Ost. B. M. 76; Hensel, Arch. für Naturg. xxviii. 128.

Herpestes parvulus, Sundeval; Temm. Esq. Zool. 110.

Hab. South Africa: Port Natal (*Sundeval*).

The skull moderate, swollen; brain-cavity ovate, contracted over the back of the orbit; nose arched; orbit incomplete behind; false grinders 2/2, front compressed, moderate, second trigonal; flesh-tooth small, broader than long, with the inner tubercle on the front edge; tubercular grinders transverse, much broader than long, the hinder about half the size of the other.

2. HELOGALE UNDULATA.

H. *nigro et rufo-flavido undulatus, subtus undique rufus; cauda corpore breviore, sine penicillo.*

Herpestes undulatus, Peters, Reise nach Mossamb. Säugeth. 114, t. 25, 1852; Gerrard, Cat. Osteol. B. M. 76; Temm. Esq. Zool. 115.

Hab. Eastern Africa: Mossambique; Quitangonka; from lat. 10° to 15° S.

Allied to *Herpestes microcephalus*, according to Temm. Esq. Zool. 118.

The grinders 5/5; the front claw much longer than the hinder; the skull ventricose, with a short nose.

Tribe 11. CYNICTIDINA.

Head short, ventricose; tail bushy, expanded laterally; claws elongate; orbit of the skull complete behind.

31. CYNICTIS.

Cynictis, Ogilby, P. Z. S. 1833, p. 48.

Body slender. Ears short, rounded. Nose truncate, with a distinct central longitudinal groove. Tail with long hairs, flattened horizontally. Legs short. Toes 5—4; front claws elongate, compressed, arched. Soles of feet partly covered with hair. Skull short and broad, ventricose. Face moderate; forehead swollen. Teeth 38; false grinders 3/3, 3/3; flesh-tooth triangular, sides subequal; tubercular grinders 2/1, 2/1.

"M. I. Geoffroy observed that the skull described by Mr. Ogilby, on which he founded his genus, had lost the front upper false grinder." —*Mag. Zool.* 1843, p. 7, note.

C. melanura, Martin, is a *Herpestes*. The type specimen which he described, now in the British Museum, has a small but distinct internal hind toe.

1. CYNICTIS PENICILLATA. B.M.

The under fur short, soft, and black.

Mangusta penicillata, Cuvier, Règ. Anim. (ed. 2); De Blainv. Ostéogr. Viverra, t. 12 (teeth).

Ichneumia albescens, I. Geoff. Mag. Zool. 1839, t. 12 (not descrip.).

Mangusta levaillantii, A. Smith, Zool. Journ.

Cynictis typicus, A. Smith, South Afr. Quart. Journ. i. 53.

C. steedmanii, Ogilby, P. Z. S. 1833, p. 49; Trans. Zool. Soc. 1835, i. 34, t. 3 (a skull); Schinz, Syn. Mamm. i. 377.

C. levaillantii, Gray, Cat. Mamm. B. M. 53; Gerrard, Cat. Ost. B. M. 77.

Meeskal, Barrow, Trav.; Swains. Lard. Ency. 159. f. 71.

Mangusta (Cynictes) penicillata, De Blainv. Ost. t. 5.

Var. redder. *Ichneumia ruber*, Geoff.

Herpestes ruber, Licht. Mus. Berlin.

Hab. South Africa (*Steedman*).

The skull short and curved; the forehead convex; brain-cavity rather swollen; upper false grinders 3/3, the first very small, the third trigonal; the flesh-tooth rather longer than broad; the tubercular grinders transverse, very short and broad, the last small.

Skull broad, the width about two-thirds the entire length; the brain-case half the entire length; orbit complete behind; forehead convex, especially between and in front of the eyes. The two front upper false grinders compressed; the third subtrigonal, with a small central internal lobe; the flesh-tooth longer than broad on the front margin; the false grinder transverse, short, and very broad, subtrigonal, widest on the outer edge, the hinder much smaller.

The skull of a younger animal very similar, but larger, and the forehead not so convex and swollen before and between the eyes.

Ichneumon rubra (Geoff. *l. c.* 139), "Very splendid ferruginous red, especially the head," is said to be *Cynictis steedmanii*, Licht.

2. CYNICTIS OGILBII. B.M.

Yellow, black-and-white pencilled; beneath whitish; chin, throat, and tip of tail white; ears reddish brown.

Cynictis ogilbii, A. Smith, S. Afr. Quart. Journ. i. 53; Illust. Z. S. Africa, Mamm. t. 16, ♂; Schinz, Syn. Mamm. i. 375.

Hab. South Africa: barren plains, north part of Graaff Reynet district and Bushman Flat (passes a great part of its time underground) (*A. Smith*).

Skull very like that of *C. levaillantii* (803 *c*); but the forehead not so convex, and the skull, though longer, is rather narrower at the zygomatic arch; the brain-cavity of the two of the same width; in the most swollen part more like 803 *a*. The flesh-tooth is similar to that of *C. levaillantii*.

3. Cynictis? fimbriata.

Fur very pale, whitish; hairs white at the base, silky, with black and white bands and a white tip; below dirty white. The black and white rings on the silky hair of the tail are broader; the lateral hairs and the tuft at the tip are tipped by an isabella band. The feet pale brown, dotted with white.

Length of body and head 11 inches, tail inches.

Herpestes fimbriatus, Temm. Esq. Zool. 112.

Hab. India (? *Temm., Mus. Leyden*).

The account of the tail would lead one to believe that this is a *Cynictis*: but the under fur of that animal, even in the very young state, is black.

4. Cynictis leptura. B.M.

Pale foxy brown, brown-pencilled; lips, chin, and tip of the tail white; tail fulvous, grizzled, with chestnut-brown hair, with a broad central chestnut-brown ring; under side yellowish white.

Cynictis lepturus, A. Smith, Illust. Zool. S. African Mamm. t. 17; Schinz, Syn. Mamm. i. 376.

C. levaillantii, var., Gerrard, Cat. Ost. B. M. 77.

Hab. South Africa, in barren places.

The skull of *Cynictis leptura* (803 *e*, A. Smith) is very like that of *C. penicillata* (803 *c*); the forehead is convex before and between the eyes, and the teeth are very similar; but the flesh-tooth is much shorter compared with the width of the front margin, more equally triangular, as the front lobe on the inner edge is longer compared with the rest of the tooth; the hinder tubercular is rather wider and more like the front one.

B. *Nose produced; under side convex, covered with short adpressed hairs, without any bald central longitudinal groove. The fur grizzled. Tail not rigid. Soles bald and slightly covered with hair.* Rhinogaleacea.

Daubenton, in the description of the Suricate (Hist. Nat. xiii. 75), observes, "Les narines ressemblent à celles du chien; mais le nez n'avait pas, comme celui du chien, un sillon qui s'étendit depuis l'entre-deux des narines jusqu'à la lèvre; cet espace était convexe." The character here described does not seem to have been remarked, since, indeed, I only accidentally discovered that Daubenton had observed it, long after I had seen its importance as a characteristic in a group of Viverridæ. The same character is found in the Mangouste figured by M. Daubenton (t. 19); but he does not notice it in his short description of a living female of that animal.

Tribe 12. Rhinogalina.

Nose short; teeth 40; *tubercular grinders* 2/2.

32. Rhinogale.

Head ovate. Nose shortly produced, convex beneath. Body elongate. Toes 5—5. Claws short, compressed, acute. Tail conical, covered with elongated hair. Skull elongate, ventricose. The orbit incomplete on the hinder edge. Teeth 40. False grinders 3/4, 3/4. Flesh-tooth triangular, broad, angle rounded; inner tubercle broad, near the middle, and occupying the greater part of the inner side. Tubercular grinders 2/1, 2/1; upper broad, transverse, rounded on the side, only half as long as wide.

This genus, in the prolongation of the nose, has some affinity to *Crossarchus* and *Ryzæna*, but the elongation is much less developed.

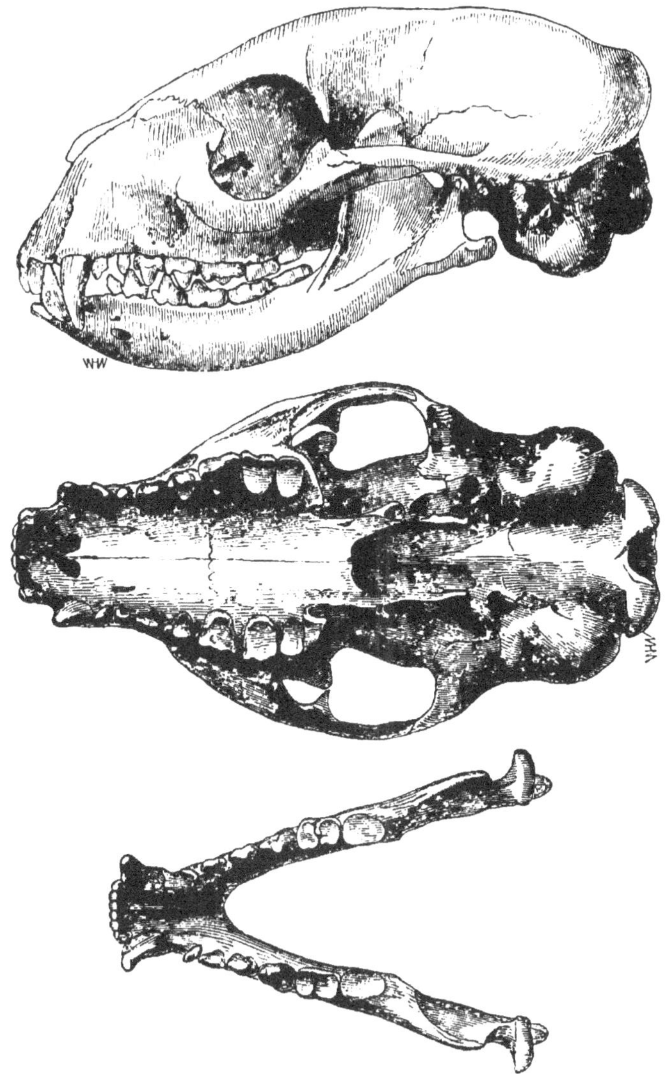

Skull of *Rhinogale melleri*.

RHINOGALE MELLERI. B.M.

Grey-brown, very minutely and closely white-speckled; the middle of the hinder part of the back with an obscure, broad, darker longitudinal streak; tail (all but the base) black; nose and feet rather brown; under fur brown.

Hab. East Africa (*Dr. Meller*).

The skull is narrow, more especially the hinder portion. The face is short and rather narrow. The forehead and crown of the head form a gradually arched line from the end of the nose to the occiput. The cavities for the temporal muscles are moderate; they meet on the crown, just over the hinder edge of the zygomatic arch, leaving a large lozenge-shaped convex forehead between the orbits. The orbits are rather small; the hinder edge incomplete. The hinder part of the palate between the temporal muscles moderately broad and short, the hinder opening being in a line with the middle of the temporal fossæ. The grinders are short, broad, and solid; the carnassier being triangular, the sides very nearly equal, the inner side being broad and rounded and placed nearly in the middle of the inner side. The tubercular grinders are oblong, transverse, with the inner side rounded and nearly as broad as the outer one; they are much worn, showing that the animal was fully adult.

33. MUNGOS.

Mungos (partly), Ogilby, MS. (see Proc. Zool. Soc. iii. 103, 1835).

Head elongate. Nose slightly produced; underside convex, with close-pressed hairs, without any central groove. Body slender. Fur rather harsh. Tail subcylindrical, covered with harsh hairs. Toes 5—5; front inner toe strong, hinder smaller. Claws strong, acute; front rather elongate, compressed, arched. Teeth 40; false grinders 3/4, 3/4; flesh-tooth triangular, as broad as long; tubercular grinders $\frac{2-2}{1-1}$, upper transverse.

Ogilby separated the genus, because in the two African species he examined there were only 2/4 false molars.

M. Temminck, with his usual want of attention to organic peculiarities, unites these animals and *Herpestes vitticollis* as a single species (see Esq. Zool. 111).

* *Back and tail grizzled.*

1. MUNGOS GAMBIANUS. B.M.

Grey, grizzled with black and grey, hair rigid, with a broad pale ring and large black tip; streak on side of neck, feet, and end of the tail black; lips, chin, and throat white; belly reddish; hair of hind limbs elongate, reddish.

Young greyer; the black tips of the hairs shorter.

Herpestes (*Mungos*) *gambianus*, Ogilby, P. Z. S. 1835, p. 102; Schinz, Syn. Mamm. i. 374; Temm. Esq. Zool. 111.

Mungos gambianus, Gray, Cat. Mamm. B. M. 50.

Hab. W. Africa; Gambia (*Rendall*).

** *Back cross-banded; tail obscurely ringed.*

2. Mungos fasciatus. B.M.

Blackish, minutely grizzled with ashy; back and rump washed with reddish, with many blackish and white cross bands; nose, feet, and ends of tail blackish.

Young paler, obscurely cross-banded.

Mungos fasciatus, Gray, Cat. Mamm. B. M.; Gerrard, Cat. Ost. B. M. 72.

Viverra ichneumon, Schreb. Säugeth. t. 116 (from Buff.).

Herpestes fasciatus, Desm. Dict. S. N. xxix. 58.

H. mungo, Desm. Mamm. 211.

H. zebra, Rüppell, Fauna Abyss. t. 9. f. 2; Schinz, Syn. Mamm. i. 371.

Ryzena suricata, Children, Clapperton's Trav. Append.

Herpestes (Mungos) fasciatus, Ogilby, P. Z. S. 1835, p. 102.

Mangusta mungo, Fisch. Syn. Mamm. 163.

Hab. Africa: Cape of Good Hope (*A. Smith*); Lake Tschad (*Clapperton*); Gambia (*Rendall*); Abyssinia (called "Gottoni") (*Rüppell*).

The not quite adult skull is rather elongate, ventricose behind, the contraction of the brain-case being in a line with the hinder part of the orbit. The orbit imperfect behind. The zygomatic arch moderately bowed out, the more convex part being nearer the hinder end. The nose tapering on the side and above, making a shelving forehead and a slightly arched crown-line. The false molars are only two on each side, there being a short space between them and the base of the canine; the second false grinder triangular, with a good-sized lobe on the inner part of the hinder edge, and with only a very rudimentary point on the hinder outer margin. The flesh-tooth triangular, the front edge being as broad as the outer one, with a large, thick, rounded inner lobe. The first tubercular grinder transverse, short, narrowed on the inner edge; the second similar, but smaller.

Length of the skull $2\frac{7}{12}$ inches; width of the brain-case 1 inch, of the zygomatic arch $1\frac{1}{2}$ inch.

Lower jaw rather slender, with a rounded angle under the condyle. The false grinders 3/3; the first compressed, sharp-edged. Tubercular grinders rather large, with two high lateral anterior and one large posterior rather high prominence.

3. Mungos adailensis.

Cinereo-flavicans, pilis nigro-fusco annulatis, vertice cerviceque nigro-schistaceis, dorso fasciis transversis obsoletis nigricantibus; abdomine dilutiore, in flavidum vergente; antepedibus obscurioribus; cauda corpore parum longiore, apice attenuata haud penicillata, dorso concolore, in ultimo triente nigra, plantis denudatis; oculis pupilla, vertico-elliptica, iride fusca.

Long. tota $22\frac{1}{2}$, caudæ 15 poll.

Herpestes adailensis, Heuglin, Peterm. Mittheil. 1861, p. 17; Nova Act. Acad. Leop. xxviii. p. 5, t. 2. f. 4 (skull).

Hab. Adail coast (*Heuglin*).

I do not see how this differs from *H. fasciatus*; but Herr Heuglin has them both in his list.

Tribe 13. Crossarchina.

Nose elongate; teeth 36; tubercular grinders 2/1.

34. Crossarchus.

Crossarchus, F. Cuv. Mamm. Lithog. iii. 47, 1825.

Head roundish. Nose elongate, much produced; the underside convex, hairy, without any central longitudinal groove; hair rigid, short, shorter on the head and throat; muffle large, callous. Pupil round. Ears rounded. Body slender. Fur harsh, with longer and more rigid hairs. Tail slightly compressed, tapering, covered with shorter hair. Toes 5—5, free; two middle toes longest; front inner toe large, hinder smaller. Soles naked. Claws rather elongated, compressed, hooked, acute, sometimes very much so. Teeth 36; false grinders 2/3, 2/3; flesh-teeth 1/1, 1/1; tubercular grinders 2/1, 2/1.

Crossarchus obscurus. B.M.

Uniform deep brown; head rather paler; hairs brown, with yellow tips.

Length of body and head 12 inches, of tail 7 inches.

Crossarchus obscurus, Cuv. R. A. i. 158; Martin, P. Z. S. 1834, p. 114 (anat.); Fischer, Syn. Mamm. 166; Schinz, Syn. Mamm. i. 379; Gerrard, Cat. Ost. B. M. 77; Temm. Esq. Zool. 117; De Blainv. Ostéogr. 49, 99, t. 12.

C. typicus, A. Smith, S. African Quart. Journ. ii. 135.

"*C. dubius*, F. Cuv.," A. Smith.

La Mangue, F. Cuvier, Mamm. Lithogr. ii. pl. 199.

Hab. Western Africa—Guinea (called "Aevisa"), living in deep holes with many openings (*Temm.*). Eastern Africa?

Crossarchus rubiginosus, Wagner, Suppl. Schreb. ii. 329. Bay brown; feet aud tip of the tail black. Length 16½ inches, of tail 12 inches.

Hab. East Indies (*Wagner*).

35. Eupleres.

Eupleres, Doyère, Ann. Sci. Nat. 1835, iv. 281; De Blainv. Ostéogr. Viverra, t. 8.

Skull ventricose, very much produced, slender, compressed; lower jaw compressed and produced in front. Nose elongate, slender, acute, proboscidiform; underside —— ?, with a small muffle. Eyes large. Ears large and triangular. Body vermiform. Legs moderate. Tarsi elongate, hairy beneath; a very slender bald streak to the heel, like *Genetta*, but not so distinct. Toes 5—5, apparently united, with scattered hairs above; thumb very short; great toe short and high up. Claws acute, semiretractile. Fur thick, formed of silky hairs, with a short close under fur. Tail elongate, cylindrical, rather tapering, covered with hair. Cutting teeth 6/6; canines small, compressed; false grinders 3, very small, compressed, far apart, the hinder with a small central internal lobe; the flesh-tooth triangular, about as long as wide, the inner lobe central; tubercular grinder trigonal, somewhat like the flesh-tooth (see De Blainv. Ostéogr. Viverra, t. 8. f. 1–4, from a young animal).

According to M. de Blainville's figure of the skull, this genus (which I have never been able to examine) is properly referred to the Viverridæ.

M. Doyère referred it to the Insectivora (see Ann. Sci. Nat. iv. 278); but, to make this alliance, he considers the front double-rooted tooth in the lower jaw a canine.

M. de Blainville, in his essay on "Mamm. Insectivores," in 'Annales Fr. et Etrang. d'Anat. et de Physiol.' ii. p. 1, justly observes, "the *Eupleres*, which has been referred to the Insectivora, on examination has proved to be allied to *Mangusta*, or to the section *Genetta* of the *Viverridæ*" (*l. c.* 37).

EUPLERES GOUDOTII.

Fur very dark brown; under fur fulvous, with black transverse streaks over the shoulder; throat and beneath whitish.

Eupleres goudotii, Doyère, Ann. Sci. Nat. 1835, iv. 281, t. 18 (animal and skull); De Blainv. Ostéogr. Viverra, t. 8 (skull); Gerrard, Cat. Ost. B. M. 71; Schinz, Syn. Mamm. i. 259.

Falanoue, Harcourt, Madagascar.

Length 12 inches, of tail 5 inches.

Hab. Madagascar, at Tamatave, in burrows (called "Falanove") (*Goudot*) (*Mus. Paris*).

36. SURICATA.

Suricata, Desm. N. Dict. H. N. xxiv. 16, 1804.

Ryzæna, Illiger, Prodr. Mamm. 1812.

Head spherical. Nose elongate, produced; underside hairy, convex, without any central groove; muffle callous; nostril long, opening on the sides. Ears rounded, nakedish internally. Body elongate; hair soft, annulated. Legs moderate. Toes 4—4; hind soles hairy. Claws long; front very long, slender, compressed, arched; anal glands two. Tail tapering, slender, covered with short hair, and rather pencilled at the tip. Teeth 36; false grinders 2/3, 2/3; flesh-teeth 1/1, 1/1; tubercular grinders 2/1, 2/1.

SURICATA ZENICK. B.M.

Grey; orbit and tip of the tail black; hinder part of the back with dark cross bands; chin, throat, and vent whitish; tail rather redder, underside lighter, under fur reddish.

Suricata zenick, Gray, Cat. Mamm. B. M. 53.
Viverra suricata, Erxl. Syst. 488.
V. tetradactyla, Pallas; Schreb. Säugeth. t. 117 (from Buffon).
Suricata viverrina, Desm. N. Dict. H. N. xxxii. 297.
S. capensis, Desm. Mamm. 214.
Viverra zenick, Gmel. S. N. i. 92 (from Sonn.).
Mangusta (Suricata) tetradactyla, De Blainv. Ostéogr. 28, t. 5. f. 12.
Ryzæna typicus, A. Smith, S. A. Q. Journ. i. 53.
R. capensis, Lesson, Mamm. 178.
R. tetradactyla, Schinz, Syn. Mamm. i. 380.
R. suricata, Fischer, Syn. Mamm. 167.
Surikate, Buffon, H. N. xiii. t. 8.
Zenic, Sonnerat, Voy. t. 92; Miller, Cim. Phys. t. 2.
Hab. South Africa (called "Meer Kat" at the Cape).

Skull short and broad, the width three-fourths the length; the brain-case broad, half the length of the skull; orbit complete behind; forehead shelving, arched; crown convex. The first upper false grinder compressed; the second subtrigonal, with a lobe on the middle of the inner side. The flesh-tooth subtrigonal, broader than long in front. The tubercular grinders transverse; the front with the inner nearly twice as broad as the outer edge; the hinder similar, but much smaller. Hinder palate-opening contracted.

14. Descriptions of Seventeen New Species of Birds from Costa Rica. By Osbert Salvin, M.A.

(Plates XXXV., XXXVI.)

The following seventeen birds I have selected, as apparently undescribed, from a collection lately sent to Mr. Godman and myself from Costa Rica, where it was made by a former collector of ours in Guatemala, Enrique Arcé, a native of the latter country. Early in the present year, with the kind assistance of Capt. J. M. Dow, Arcé left Guatemala, and, after forwarding a small collection from the Pacific slope, crossed over to the valleys of the eastern coast; and it is from this latter district that the following birds have been principally selected. The remainder of the collection comprises many of the rare types described a few years back by Cabanis, and also several Humming-birds, M. Warszewicz's discoveries in Veragua. I am now acquainted with about 304 species (mostly *Passeres*) from this country, no less than about 65 of which have been described by various authors as new, and which have not as yet been found beyond the limits of Costa Rica or the immediately adjoining province of Veragua. Arcé is continuing his labours; and I hope ere long that through him and Dr. von Franzius, from whom Prof. Baird of Washington is receiving collections, that this most interesting country will be thoroughly explored. In determining these species, I acknowledge the kind aid of Mr. Sclater and Mr. Gould, and the advantage of free access to their collections.

www.ingramcontent.com/pod-product-compliance
Lightning Source LLC
Chambersburg PA
CBHW021522270326
41930CB00008B/1052

* 9 7 8 3 7 4 1 1 3 0 4 8 9 *